MW01008523

TECHNICAL
TRADING
MASTERY

TECHNICAL TRADING MASTERY

Chris Vermeulen

Carpenter's Son Publishing

Technical Trading Mastery for Traders & Investors

Copyright © 2014 Technical Traders Ltd.

The three traits speculators must learn to manage within themselves are confidence, fear, and aggressiveness.

Larry Williams

CONTENTS

ACKNOWLEDGMENTS

To my amazing wife, Kristen, for her persistent optimism and patience during the writing of the book. To my 4-year-old daughter, Mirabelle, and 2-year-old son, Ben. It was a joy to have you both by my side, and I thank you for allowing me to share the computer with you throughout this project.

A special thanks to my mom, dad and sister who provided their love and encouragement.

A big thank you goes to my editor, Tammy Kling. Thank you for all the great insight and recommendations, and thank you for making my words so much more readable.

Thanks to those who I learned from and those who inspired me over the years: Larry Williams, John Murphy, Martin J. Pring, Stan Weinstein, John Ehlers, Michael Swanson, Brian McAboy, Brennan Basnicki, Jack

Schwager, Bob Baird, Richard L. Peterson, Tony Jeary, Mark Magnacca and many more.

To all of the followers of my daily videos and articles at www.thegoldandoilguy.com, thank you for the support and all the questions which I hope I have answered within this book.

I know this methodology will help hundreds of thousands of traders and investors succeed in the busy and fast-paced financial markets of the world. Much success!

FOREWORD

Business is a results contest; so is trading.

You're reading this book because you want to become a successful trader and you want to continue to get the very best results. My client and friend, Chris Vermeulen of Technical Traders Ltd., is the absolute best in his industry because he is committed to stakeholder (his mentees) results. For years he has studied, focused and executed the very best practices in technical trading. He has walked the walk, and he's also taught and advised many others along the way. When Chris came to me for business coaching, his goals were to get even better and to gain a higher level of mastery. We focused on these three key areas to get results: clarity, focus and execution.

These are the principles I convey to the world's top CEOs, entrepreneurs and companies. With clarity, you are absolutely clear about what you want (your vision). With focus, you are able to remove many distractions in order to focus on your HLAs (High Leverage Activities), which are what matter most. With execution, you make it all happen.

Clarity, focus and execution will be a big part of what you learn from Chris within these pages. As you read and study, you'll grow your trading expertise and achieve results that will take you to higher levels!

As a trader, you want results, and not just any results. You have got to achieve the best results possible. Chris, in the following pages, walks you through years of study and refinement in simple, easy to understand segments. You absorb, test, focus and move into mastery as a trader.

Always keep learning, and get there faster from following those who have traveled ahead and know what's coming. For trading, Chris is the guy!

Tony Jeary,
Coach to the World's Top CEOs and High Achievers
(often referred to as The RESULTS Guy™).

CHAPTER 1

INTRODUCTION

When I was 16, I found a booklet in the mailbox about how fortunes could be made trading the futures market, and it immediately intrigued me. It was written by a guy I'd not yet heard of, Larry Williams. Yet even as a kid I already loved the feeling of making money, and I was great at working with numbers. On top of that, I also loved the adventure of taking measured risks, so when I saw the book, I devoured it.

I read that booklet four times before I approached my dad and asked him if we could start trading futures together. He wasn't interested in this type of business because he had his own successful businesses already, but he was supportive. He told me to learn more and go from there. I did, and I got bit by the trading bug, big time.

When I went to college, I started and ran my own successful landscaping business every summer, and I started saving that money to start trading.

I became addicted to watching the stock market on CNBC from my dorm room and learned more and more about trading. It fueled the fire, and on the day I turned 18, I asked my dad to co-sign on a trading account with $2,000 I had saved up over the summer. A week later I was ready to rock and roll and trade from my dorm room!

Just a couple of months later, I had turned $2000 into $8000 (trading stocks because I was not approved for futures yet, nor did I have the money required for it), and I was on my way. I knew I'd found my passion and purpose.

What about you?

WHY ARE YOU READING THIS BOOK?

Chances are you already know a bit about trading and are ready to understand the technical aspects of it. Or maybe you're already somewhat of an expert and want to learn more.

Understanding what drives you will help you establish your goals and outcomes. We seek to learn because we want something. Maybe it's the challenge of achievement or maybe it's the joy of seeing profit or building something, or perhaps it's as simple as watching your bank account grow. Having wealth is power because it gives you freedom. But creating wealth is even more powerful.

My journey evolved from learning to executing trades and continually researching and perfecting the technical aspects of the process. But on each step of the way, I was interested in understanding more because I was passionate about trading.

In 2001 I started sharing my trades and analysis online because other traders told me I had great analytical skills and a gift for mentoring. Now my journey continues with TheTechnicalTraders.com INNER-Market Analysis Signal Tools, a system derived from years of trial and error, experience, and various processes and methodologies. I decided I wanted to share what I've learned with others in order to help them be successful at trading.

WHAT'S YOUR GOAL?

For me, trading offers freedom. I grew up in an entrepreneurial family, where both parents had their own businesses and worked hard at being the best and staying on top of their game. If you've ever been an entrepreneur, you know that sometimes you win and sometimes you lose, but your destiny is always in your own hands. You've got what a lot of other people don't have—independence.

As a result of my parents owning their own businesses, we were able to travel, go on extravagant vacations and spend a lot of time together as a family.

Maybe you want to have the freedom of owning your own business, or perhaps you just want to set aside some money to learn the business of trading. Or perhaps you really want to grow your nest egg and earn money for something big. Either way, the information in this book is designed to get you up to speed on trading in the shortest time frame possible.

In my career as a full time trader and coach, I've met traders that were confused by all the different investment vehicles, tools, and indicators available. They had all the knowledge they needed, but no one told them how to apply it to themselves and real trading. But application (action) makes the difference. It's the difference between winning and not doing anything at all! What's knowledge if we don't use it?

I've been trading and coaching others how to trade for years, and freedom was a big driver in my motivation for entering the business. I wanted to be free to work from home, an island, or a mountain. I wanted to avoid offices and suits. I wanted to avoid bosses who would require things of me that I didn't feel inspired to do. I just wanted independence.

I started watching stock quotes, and I realized how big the profit potential was if I could just cut out a small piece of the markets' movements each month. I knew there would be obstacles to conquer, however, in order to achieve success consistently.

In the pages to follow, I'll teach you how to keep it simple.

Personally, I don't think trading needs to be complicated. Keeping things simple is the key to repeatable success. I've studied many of the world's top traders, and they only use a few basic strategies in combination with simple tools and indicators.

This does not mean trading is simple. There is a lot of room for failure when it comes to self-discipline and trade execution. There isn't any trading method that's 100 percent bullet proof. All systems and strategies have losing trades, but through the years our process is replicable and effective. It has taken several individuals to exciting new levels in their trading!

My goal in this book is to bring you a solid understanding of market dynamics so you can use my proven strategy or develop your own based on a comprehensive understanding of market structure and how it moves. Any strategy based on a thorough understanding of market tendencies should provide a disciplined trader with profits. I will help you figure these things out and get you trading like a pro as quickly as possible.

The most effective way to become successful as a trader is to learn directly from someone who has already made the mistakes and been through the struggle!

BE A MASTER, IN JUST
A MATTER OF MONTHS

In 2001 I started sharing my market analysis online through an email newsletter, which fast-tracked a trader's learning curve from beginner to advanced within a few months.

In 2008, I decided I wanted to make the learning curve of reading the markets through the use of technical analysis even easier, faster and more automated!

I had lived and breathed trading, studied strategies and implemented them with success. Now it was time to develop a way to help others do the same thing.

After countless hours of analysis, and with the help of multiple programmers to help convert my knowledge, expertise and strategies into a real-time automated technical analyst, I was on my way. I created a system that I use today, and it works.

The system does all the time-consuming number crunching so that an individual can accurately identify the current market trend. It shows when prices are overbought or oversold, spots trend reversals, identifies sideways choppy markets, and actively pinpoints short-term highs and lows. It does this all while providing trading advice like position sizes based on the market volatility, entry signals (long or short), profit-taking levels, and protective stops.

When you use the tools inside these pages, you'll learn things like how to anticipate the markets entry and exit points ahead of others. You'll learn how to get skilled at recognizing market movements, and how to utilize technical analysis to fuel your trading strategy.

You don't need to know and trade everything. The key is to find a few simple strategies that work for you and master them. Knowing what strategy is best for you is critical for success, as it must fit with your personality, available time, self-discipline and current knowledge of the financial market. Read on, and enjoy the journey!

THE TRADERS LITMUS PAPER TEST

Answer the statements below using a Yes or No answer. Add up the total number of Yes answers at the bottom.

- Do you have a detailed trading plan to work from?

- Clear set-up criteria for each trade and adjustment?

- Are you tired of watching your account decline during market down turns and bear markets?

- Do you have a detailed investment plan to work from?

- Use a hard protective stop for every trade?

- Have trading rules you don't stick too?

- Do you have a routine that gets you back on track when you're trading is off?

- Do you lack the preparation for your trading day?

- Do you not keep track of all your trades?

- Do your losing trades typically outweigh your winners?

- Do you have having several winning trades, followed by larger, crash and burn types of trades?

- Do you experience hesitation, apprehension, uncertainty or fear when you are about to trade?

- Do you double down after a losing streak or when you're losing to regain profits faster?

- Have you ever gone into the "I don't care" mode and watched your money disappear when in a trade?

- After losing a large amount of money, are you emotionally challenged on every trade after that loss?

- Were you successful in another profession and find trading is affecting your confidence and ego?

- Do you lose sleep over your trading?

- Do you see your trade set-up and still hesitate to enter?

- Are you exiting a trade too quickly instead of waiting for the trade to mature to its full potential?

- Are a high percentage of your trades defensive?

- Do you logically know what to do in a trade but find you are not taking the actions you should?

- Do you have anxiety when trading and enter too soon?

Total the number of Yes's _____

IF YOU HAVE MORE THAN SIX YES ANSWERS, THEN YOU NEED A TRADING PHILOSOPHY, A TRADING BUSINESS PLAN, AND NEW TRADING STRATEGIES. THIS BOOK WILL HELP YOU ACCOMPLISH EACH OF THESE THINGS.

CHAPTER 2

UNDERSTANDING YOUR GOALS

When you begin trading, there are a lot of questions. And with all the information out there, it can be hard to filter through and decide where to start. Setting goals can help, but often novice traders set the wrong type of goals. Your initial goals should be based on things to help you learn to eventually make money. But making money, however, should not be the main goal.

Instead, opt to make your initial goals about learning the process and emulating traits of successful traders. In order to become successful at trading, understand who you are. Are you an investor? A swing trader? A momentum or day trader? These are all of the things I'll help you discover in the chapters to follow. Understanding your goal is the first step to achieving it.

Once you do, you can master the trading strategy and rules that fit your personality and style of trading. Only then will the money and profits follow!

MAKE YOUR GOALS ABOUT THE PROCESS, NOT RESULTS

Initially, traders want to make goals about numbers. They generally make statements like: "I will make 1 percent per day on my $30,000 capital" as a day-trading example, or "I will make 30 percent per year" as an investing example. In the beginning, I probably made the same bold statements. I went through the frustrating process of learning the technical aspects of trading, and it took me years (and thousands of dollars in learning and courses) to figure it out. In these pages, you'll learn from my experiences and years of research and application.

Setting a specific dollar amount to achieve isn't the goal. While it might seem simple, the reality is that in order to get to certain percentage or dollar targets, you will need to refine your approach, knowledge and discipline.

By just plunging into the market and expecting to make a certain amount of money, your goal becomes almost impossible to reach over the long-term. These types of goals require that the trader actually know the capabilities (and limitations) of the trading plan they are employing; not think they know, but actually know. It's a technical process. This book is designed to give you extreme focus in order to learn the skill of Technical Trading.

WHAT'S YOUR STRATEGY?

As a trader, you have to have an understanding of the potential and pitfalls of the strategy you are employing. Based on the method being used, it may be impossible to reach a dollar or percentage goal, but the method still could be valid and provide a good return. Therefore, the trader must either abandon that method, find a new one in an attempt to find a higher yield, then master one strategy to the best of their ability. They then should find or create another strategy that adds some diversification and added income to their trading through the use of different time frames or underlying investment (or both).

For many traders, this becomes an endless cycle of abandoning strategy after strategy and never being able to adhere to a plan. If you do not settle with one system that works and grow your knowledge to master more profitable strategies, you are in for a long and frustrating journey.

It's certainly okay to have a motivating dream in mind. But don't make the dream the goal; make the process of understanding a technical strategy the goal. Your dream might be to earn an extra $1,000, $5,000 or even 20,000+ a month, which can certainly be achieved with a couple of simple, yet well-planned, trading strategies. Or maybe you just want to earn enough to pay for a vacation once a year, buy a boat or purchase a new car. All of that is possible, of course. But in order to achieve those results, there is a process. It's like training to become a professional athlete. It requires dedication and a commitment to the technical process.

When starting out, do not set goals for exact income profit or income level; instead, focus on learning a process that will allow you to make money consistently. When you do this, it will remove any unrealistic expectations and replace them with the desire to get good at trading and understand how to get consecutive, repeatable results. The financial market does not make profitable trading easy. With the proper knowledge, tools and discipline, we can create profitable trading strategies for virtually any investment and time frame. But keep in mind, the market at best only allow us a small edge that we can use to turn a profit.

As we all know, it takes money to make money. Many of the top performing and consistent trading strategies only pull 0.5 percent to five percent in profits per month. It may not sound like much, and to be honest, it's not. But when you apply different trading vehicles like leveraged exchange traded funds, options or futures, these low-risk, high-probability trades generate very exciting returns. So focus on the process and attempt to perfect that, and the results will happen on their own. If you attempt to achieve results without perfecting the process, the markets will likely continually take your money!

TECHNICAL ANALYSIS

To become a great trader, you must find proven trading strategies to use. Results will not come instantly. Most businesses take quite a bit of time before profits come, and many, many more businesses fail completely. Trading is no different. Results will not come instantly, and if they do, it is likely due to luck. Without understanding how the markets truly work, the results are based on chance, not skill.

Here are three goals. These may not seem like goals at all, but they are in fact and are very hard to do. Even professional traders battle with these throughout their careers. If you focus on mastering these areas from the very beginning, positive results are more likely to ensue.

GOAL #1: ALWAYS HAVE A PLAN

In business school, you are taught that in order to start a business, you need a business plan. Trading is a business. Therefore, every time you trade, you must be trading according to a well thought-out and calculated plan.

Your plan should include:

- Laying the Foundation
- You, the Successful Business Owner
- You, the Successful Trader
- Your Successful Trading System(s)
- Ensuring the Financial Success of Your Trading Business
- Making Your Success Easily Sustainable
- Bringing the Business Plan Together
- Living Independently Once You're Free

The plan must be concise, complete and transformative. Details like outlining the markets that will be traded, risk parameters, if filters will be used on trade signals, what constitutes a trade and exit signal, position size, how often you want to be trading and the method in which you are going to use to generate signals must be planned. For example, do you use technical analysis or fundamental data, and how you will trade those signals? Do you want to manually place each trade or use a system to have it automatically traded in your account for you?

Therefore, the goal here is to create a complete plan for trading the markets ... before ever making a trade! Your comprehensive business plan will transform you into an entirely different person, ready for a life of true independence through trading and genuine entrepreneurship. Your tested and proven trading strategies will be the products which generate you income.

GOAL #2: LEARN NOT TO TRADE

Learn how to observe, strategize and plan. Keep the emotion out of it, and focus on technical rules and procedures instead. This will help you learn not to trade reactively and not to trade out of an errant desire to reach a financial goal. When a specific dollar amount is the goal, traders will push to achieve that goal even when opportunities are not present.

The market does not present statistically probable trading opportunities at all times! This is a hard truth to learn, but there are often times when you will be far better off sitting on your hands or watching TV than trading. This does not sit well with most people; they want to continually be doing something. In the markets, this can slowly (or quickly) erode profits that came during good trading times. When, and when not, to trade is covered in detail later in this book, but know that many highly successful traders only have their money in the markets 20 to 30 percent of the time. When they are not in the market, they are sitting and waiting in cash for the next high probability trade.

GOAL #3: KEEP IT SIMPLE—AVOID COMPLEX TRADING STRATEGIES

A complex strategy can be very alluring. Many people believe that because something is complex, it is more likely to work than something that is simple. But that is simply not true here. Avoid getting too fancy with your analysis and trading strategies. As you progress, avoid the desire to make a winning trading plan more complex. Usually this only results in destroying the long-term profitability of it.

The goal here is to avoid constant tinkering in order to improve performance, and to avoid continually switching markets, strategies or analysis methods. Stick to a plan. If it occasionally needs to be reworked a bit, that is fine. But keep the revisions simple, and avoid getting overly complex.

Trading is a skill-based occupation, and a mastery of your trading strategies is the one skill that you must have to be in control of your financial future.

- Ensure that your system is proper, complete and trade-able (Key to Success)

- Remove any doubts by properly confirming your system's TRUE potential for profit, then solidifying your execution of it (Keys to Consistency)

- Optimize your trading system in a very calculated and business-like manner (Key to Security)

The three critical skills Trading System Mastery includes:

Trading Method Systemization—You'll have the pro-per perspectives, process and techniques to take your trading method and systemize it THE RIGHT WAY so that it is very 'trade-able', complete and most importantly, REPEATABLE for easy and consistent execution. This one is HUGE because a primary problem traders have is that their system is missing certain elements and/or qualities that make it difficult to execute consistently.

Trading System Confirmation—You'll learn exact-ly how to properly confirm the performance of your trading system so that you have the confidence you need to stick to it. When it comes to 'discipline' problems like 'hesitation,' nothing will help you more than the unshakable confidence that comes from PROPER confirmation. When you replace your fears with that kind of confidence, sticking to your system becomes the natural response and EASY.

Trading System Optimization—Whether it is sim-ply to make improvements or because circumstances force you to, you will know how to adapt quickly and confidently, always moving forward. Nothing is worse than having things change, your system no longer working, and not knowing what to do. In '08 and '09, many traders blew out their accounts, and they were done with trading because they were lost. Never again be nervous when the markets get turned upside down. Instead, be in the minority that is thriving!

Focus on only one market, and use only a couple of strategies when first starting out. I focus on the S&P 500 index and use a few simple strategies to generate a weekly and monthly income.

"It's better to be really good at one thing than average at a bunch of things"

THE BOTTOM LINE

When starting out, be a niche trader and focus on one strategy and investment at time. Your goals should focus on mastering the process of becoming a successful trader.

Remember to have a positive mental attitude while you are on this journey. You must truly believe that you have the requisite abilities and skills to achieve your goals. If you believe in the back of your mind that your goals are unrealistic or that you don't have the ability to achieve them, you will succumb to self-doubt and be likely to give up.

In the next chapter, we'll talk about the mindset of a good trader, positive self-talk, and really define who you are. All of those things, combined with your personality traits, values, available time and desire, will allow you to become a better trader over time. Self-awareness, is a critical component of succeeding at any business. Understand your limitations! Don't handicap yourself, set realistic expectations, and most of all, stay committed to the process. Stay committed to learning and to making it happen! Be committed to believing in yourself.

Lying within you is a complex interplay between goal-setting and your belief in your ability to achieve those goals. If you set goals that are too high, you will give up when you start encountering setbacks. It's better to set goals that are within your grasp. When you set a goal that lies within your grasp, you will work diligently to achieve it. You will feel a sense of accomplishment each step of the way, and you will feel enthusiastic about continuing toward your vision.

CHAPTER 3

Trading with Intention— The Life of a Technical Trader

There is an interesting thing that happens in our lives when we decide on goals. We feel crisper and sharper. Our senses are honed. We begin to measure the world by a different barometer.

Most of us are accustomed to mundane goals and how to measure them:

Lose weight—Step on a scale and compare previous weight.

Save for a big ticket item—Skip smaller indulgences and stockpile cash.

Start a trading career—Trade and watch your account grow.

And we are also familiar with the (negative) flip side of our intentions:

> Forget this whole idea—It's too much work, and I want that rich carrot cake NOW! I want to buy new music, apps, clothes, concert tickets or other distractions and satisfactions.

Trading with intention is hard to do. Too often we interpret it as unreasonable quantities of patience and denial. And it seems especially hard if our goals are not crystal clear and vague; make a lot of money, create more free time, quit my job. The intentional trader needs to define what their reason for trading is and to have a clear understanding of the realities of their goals. By this I mean to define "lots of money" and "free time." What does it look like? What will it do for you? Why do you want it?

We tend to think of intention as focused will. We see it as having the right stuff, and as having the sternness and self-control to consistently mold our trading to a larger, and usually delayed, goal. But sometimes focused will is simply not enough. It is not only because we are human and filled with emotions, though that's certainly part of it, but because we tend to operate using only a small part of our energies. We get so used to acting on the surface of our lives, so used to coping with the myriad demands of trading, work, family and friends that we too often forget to knock on the doors of our inner strengths and abilities and say: hey, wake up, I need some help.

The whole point of having some sort of guidance system (clearly defined trading method) is that you have support and confidence., This way, you don't have to rely on sheer willpower to keep you on track and to help you remember. By boosting your emotional, self-appreciating, and psychological strength, you reduce the load of self-discipline needed to execute trades properly.

Successful traders follow a technical system, and they trade with intention. As I've researched, implemented, tried, tested, proven, and created trading strategies that are repeatable over the years, I've learned what works and what doesn't. Of course, total accountability for trading lies with the individual trader, and you can only teach so much. Eventually it is up to the individual.

Education, training, practice, experience, and the patience to try not to reinvent the wheel are all things a trader needs to do to become successful. Success in just about anything, whether it is business or athletics, is not about luck or timing. It's about preparation, discipline and proper attitude. Are you committed to the process? Will you be disciplined? Do you have what it takes to execute a strategy, even if it seems simple, repetitive or unemotional?

Much has been written about investing and how to become successful at doing it. Knowing this, it's not surprising that there has been a plethora of abbreviated lists of the essentials of what it takes to become a successful trader. But it is always good to continually review the basics. A first line of strategy in helping to reduce risk and increase success is to transfer the well-known into the well-implemented. But, as with most academic subjects, it's easy to "talk the talk," but it is a different matter to "walk the walk."

CHARACTERISTICS OF SUCCESSFUL TRADERS

Many investors take actions that aren't in their best self-interest. They make irrational trades; they trade based on emotion rather than logic; they hold on to a losing position due to their unwillingness to admit they made a bad trade; they trade based on greed or panic ... and so on. The list is endless.

Successful traders, on the other hand, all have a few things in common. Developing these characteristics and habits will help make you a successful trader, too.

1) Successful Traders Set Goals

Successful traders tend to be incredibly goal-oriented. Why? Most people perform at their best when they are reaching for a clear goal. There are three basic qualities that make up a clear goal:

- **The goal must be realistic.** If your goal is to double your money every month, it's not realistic.

- **The goal must be attainable.** Just like with a realistic goal, an attainable goal must be within your current capabilities. The best goals are short-term goals; make your first goal a small one and then continue to increase your goals as you experience success. World-class sprinters don't start by thinking of winning the Olympics.

- **The goal must be measurable.** Goals that aren't precise, and therefore can't be quantified or measured, aren't really goals at all. If your goal is to be wealthy, that's great. But what does "wealthy" mean? Our guess is that your definition of "wealth" will change as your net worth increases. If you can't define your goal and measure your progress toward it, then you have no way of assessing your progress. You therefore cannot make changes to your techniques and strategies that allow you to reach your goal.

Successful traders set goals, and they also are confident they can reach their goals. Confidence is a key to staying rational, logical and disciplined. Starting with small, realistic goals will help build confidence in yourself and your abilities.

2) **Successful traders realize that success can come at any level**

Whether you're a beginning trader, a trader with some experience or someone who makes his or her living strictly from trading, you can be successful. Many people think they have to have significant capital, or years of experience, to trade successfully. That's not true. (It's also true that if you don't stay disciplined, focused and rational, you'll end up as a losing trader, regardless of your level of "expertise.")

All successful traders started as small investors; they didn't trade more than they could safely risk, they learned from their mistakes, and they developed a system that worked for them and fit their personal styles. We have not defined different strategies for different "levels" of traders in this book because the principles are the same: logical, focused and disciplined trading creates success.

3) Successful Traders Specialize

It is simply not possible to understand and stay in touch with everything that occurs in all the types of investment vehicles and markets across the world. While some traders have developed systems that allow them to trade in multiple venues (for instance, in different stock markets around the world), most traders specialize in a particular type of investment and in a particular market. You may enjoy trading in commodity futures; that enjoyment will help you focus and stay in touch with those market events. Whatever you decide to specialize in, it should be your main focus and where the majority of your trades take place.

If you aren't interested in currency trading, for example, don't trade in it; your lack of knowledge and motivation will cause you to lose focus and make mistakes. Successful traders tend to specialize; they pick an area to gain in-depth knowledge of. They follow it closely, learning from past trends and patterns and from their own trades. If you're a beginning trader, we recommend focusing narrowly on a particular investment vehicle and market. Learn all you can in that area, both about the market and about yourself, before you move into other investment types.

4) Successful Traders Take Losses in Stride

No one likes to lose, but losing is a fact of life for traders. The key is to limit your losses and maximize your successes.

A losing trade is not a failure. It isn't a reflection of you or of your overall judgment. (If it was possible to be right every time, we'd all be rich.) The only way a losing trade is truly a failure is if you aren't willing to take the loss, without hesitation, and move on to find winning trades. By accepting that they've made a losing trade and getting out of the position, successful traders focus on making money – not on being right all the time.

Many traders feel they don't want to "lose" money on any trade, and they stay in losing positions in the hopes that it will recover to at least the break-even point. There are three problems with this approach:

• The position may never recover to the break-even point.

• Holding on to a losing position ties up capital that could be placed into winning trades.

• Holding on to a losing position is an example of unfocused trading and a lack of discipline.

Successful traders are willing to take small losses. If you aren't willing to take small losses or don't have the discipline to take small losses, don't trade.

5) Successful Traders Stay Focused During Rapid Swings

Most of us were raised to think that it takes years of hard work to acquire wealth. That viewpoint doesn't apply to trading in the markets; you can make thousands of dollars in minutes under the right circumstances. Successful traders understand that money can be made or lost extremely quickly, and they stay calm and rational.

Why is that attitude important? Let's say you've made several thousand dollars over the course of an hour by trading futures contracts. You're thrilled and excited, and you may lose your composure and start making irrational trades.

You may stay in the position longer than you should, for one of two reasons:

• You think the market will keep going up, and you don't want to limit your gains.

• The market falls, but you don't want admit the market move could be over, so you hold on in hopes your position will rally.

If you accept and understand that huge amounts of money can be made in a short period of time, you are more likely to stay disciplined in your trading.

Successful traders take their gains in stride, no matter how large. They quickly move to protect their positions by setting stops, which lock in gains on a portion of their position to reduce their risk and market exposure. Successful traders stay rational and disciplined in the face of rapid gains or losses because they understand the nature of trading.

6) Successful Traders Stay Flexible

Staying flexible requires that you stay detached and unemotional about your trades. No matter how strongly you feel about your analysis of a position or a trade, you have to be willing to change that opinion and act quickly if necessary. Detachment is your friend.

Successful traders realize that bad trades reduce the gains made from past trades and also affect potential gains from future trades. Successful traders change their minds quickly and easily, and they are not concerned about whether they were "right" or "wrong." They're concerned with maximizing their gains and minimizing their losses. And to minimize losses, they have to be willing to quickly change their minds. Remember, the more flexible you are, the more successful you will be.

7) Successful Traders Don't Leap Before They Look

One of the most common mistakes inexperienced traders make is to trade when they see an opportunity they think might be too good to miss. Jumping into a position based on a hunch, or on the belief that you may be missing an opportunity, is no different than gambling. Almost every investor at one time or another has felt a rush of greed or enthusiasm for a trade based solely on the desire not to miss out on a great opportunity.

Successful traders practice self-discipline, and they apply skill and logic to their trading. They learn every day, and they use what they know to make intelligent decisions on every trade. Successful traders don't worry about missing out; they focus on making intelligent decisions.

WHAT YOU FOCUS ON IS WHAT YOU TEND TO GET

The human mind gathers information about the outside world through the uses of the senses. The mind recognizes the information and then processes it. It then responds to that information with a whole host of beliefs, which are both unconscious and subconscious.

Based upon a person's motivations and interpretations of what is taking place, he carries out an action. The key is that actions that people take are based upon their own set of associations with what is going on in the world outside of them. These associations are based upon past experiences and a person's beliefs about himself and the task at hand. The world consists of inputs that make people feel and respond accordingly.

To relate this to trading, winning traders and losing traders experience the trading environment differently. It makes them feel different, and as a result, their actions consistently vary. In psychological terms, they interpret the market differently because they have a separate belief system in the way that they see themselves relative to the stock market. This is an important awareness tool as you begin to understand how to refine, modify and execute with the right mindset as opposed to the wrong one. Your mindset and belief systems make the difference between being a successful trader or an unsuccessful one. Belief statements that traders might make:

WINNING TRADERS

1. The markets provide an opportunity.

2. The markets exist to give me profits.

3. If I get stopped out, then I have to reevaluate the trade.

4. If the market doesn't do what I expect, then I must reconsider.

5. I'll take it one trade at a time.

6. I don't have to be perfect, I just have to do my best.

7. Losing sometimes is part of the process of making money.

8. Trading is a game, and I know I can win.

9. Every setback provides me with new market information.

10. I can wait for an opportunity to come.

LOSING TRADERS

1. I must be in the market now.

2. If I lose on this trade, I am a loser.

3. If I wait for my trading rules, I'll miss out.

4. If I get stopped out, I have bad luck.

5. I can't lose money.

6. The market makers got me again.

7. I'm an idiot, how could I lose money?

8. What will they think when I tell them I lost money on this one?

9. The stock market is rigged.

10. It's impossible to get a good order execution.

These different beliefs create different characteristics of winning and losing traders.

WINNERS

- Get pleasure from trading the market as an end in itself

- Are not motivated primarily by money

- Are confident that they can make money in the market

- Are not afraid to take a loss

- Are patient and wait for opportunities

- Use a highly planned strategy

- Are well-prepared and have done their homework

- Measure the risk/reward ratio of every trade

- Keep position size manageable with risk limits

LOSING TRADERS

- Never define a loss

- Are locked into a narrow belief system

- Hesitate to make a trade

- Do not stick to a system

- Trade by whim

- Trade by emotion

- Have no consistent strategy

- Do not practice risk management

- Are more interested in proving themselves right then being a success

- Trade a large percentage of their accounts to try and hit a grand slam on every trade.

Financial markets are structured in such a way that make it very difficult for someone to approach them with a confident psyche. That is why it is so difficult for most people to make money by trading in them. Almost all environments—the workplace, family and friends—provide external forces that limit a person's behavior. They provide a set of rules of what is right and wrong, and what actions are to be rewarded or punished. This is not true for the stock market.

It's absolutely critical to get into the proper frame of mind before starting your journey. If you looked at the belief systems of losing traders above and identified with them, it's time to make a change. You have got to change your mindset belief system so that it mirrors the attitude of winning traders. If you know you can't, you may be in the wrong business.

One of the things that makes trading so amazing to me is that once you know what you are doing in terms of analyzing the market and managing your trades, life is SO GOOD and simple. I can look at the charts and in five minutes tell you if there is a potential trade or a position that may need to be managed on that day. If there is a trade setup, my system alerts me so they come to my email and cell phone. If there is a possible trade, I will stay close the computer to monitor things and take action when needed. My stress level is VERY low when it comes to trading because I have systems in place. My systems keep my mind clear on the outcome and on what I should be doing each step of the way.

You are about to see the financial markets in a whole new light, and likely with an entirely different focus than you've experienced so far. Up until now, you may have been on "The Quest," searching for that one thing that works and that you can rely upon.

Odds are that you have already had a profitable trading idea, but perhaps you weren't able to realize it. Maybe you 'feel' pretty strongly that you've got a solid system, but you haven't been able to settle down and trade it the way you know you should. Up until now, it is possible that you've had this feeling of desperation constantly hanging over your head, and you have hoped that your next idea will be your ticket to freedom. Or perhaps you are just starting out in the process and are not that well-versed yet in where you need to go and what steps you need to take. Congratulations, you've arrived at a great starting point. You can do it!

CREATE A HABIT OF POSITIVE SELF TALK

Truly trading with intention involves engaging all of your energies and strengths, not merely your mental ones.

It means activating your inner strengths and engaging in positive self talk and into action. It means both affirming what you want and being satisfied with being on the journey. It means honoring your intention, even if you have not yet reached your goal. Trading with intention means pushing your comfort zone, but it also means appreciating every nuance of trading and appreciating yourself for being conscious as you do it. It means recognizing that the act of envisioning that moment of connecting with your intention counts as much as executing the trades which your system generates. The first step to making your trading career successful is imagining it so. Envision yourself as a trader who takes all trades within your system with a positive attitude and who is experiencing the rewards of dedication.

Trading with intention means persistently and actively affirming your goals. This is so that you don't forget or diminish their value when you face a challenge, and so that you are intimately connected with both process and outcome.

YOUR COMMITMENT TO THE PROCESS

Make a change in how you relate to this process. Instead of merely measuring the outer barometers (ticks, points, dollars, account size), focus on your inner ones. Commit regular time with yourself in evaluating the more subtle contexts of your trading. This does not mean fretting over why you went short into a line of support, or thinking how impossible it seems to get ahead. Instead, it means looking how you truly approach your trading as it relates to your goals and giving yourself a regular report card. And, as hard as it is for some of us to do, it means giving yourself a pat on the back when you honor your intention, even if you haven't yet reached your final goals.

Stop muttering to yourself, and stop chastising yourself for lapses. Close your eyes, envision yourself at your goal, and take a few deep breaths of success. Put your energy into reinforcing your trust that you truly can do this. A part of you is already where you want to be. It just takes time to open up and take the next step.

Keep reminding yourself that each time you affirm your intention and each time you commit to the process, you are actually doing something positive. The process itself clears away your fears. It fills you with a new sense of what trading can be for you and your family, and it tells you why you can do it if you really want to. Don't just wish you could trade with intention. Take the first step and trust where you will lead yourself.

THE CORRECT PATH LEADS TO RELIEF

Relief is what you will feel because now you will have the skill-set, strategy and know-how to execute a consistently profitable strategy.

Once you have reached that milestone of KNOWING that you're 'Okay,' you now enjoy a feeling of security.

You finally know that you can relax and settle down. You have a certain peace of mind about you that people notice, and they may even comment on it.

Your time and energy are now focused simply expanding your capabilities as a trader and increasing your revenues and accounts. You become the type of trader that can, in a calculated and business-like fashion, take ANY trading strategy or method, construct a working trading system based on it, optimize it and validate it properly. When you take it to the markets, you do so with a well-founded confidence that suits you. You know that you can trade it well, and you have a reasonable expectation that it will meet your financial goals.

As you go through this process, you become one of those traders that has the skills, tools and know-how to adapt quickly and confidently when the economic climate or market mood changes. You will also be able to broaden your portfolio of systems to maximize your profit potential as a trader.

It's about the thought process. If you're committed to becoming a professional golfer, for instance, you'd have to think like a professional golfer. You'd have to eat, breathe and sleep golf, but you'd also have to know the technical aspects of golf in order to progress and win. Golf is a perfect example because it's a mental game. When you swing a golf club for the first time, the instructor corrects you and tells you to swing in such a way that feels unnatural, yet it turns out to be the proper form. It's not like swinging a baseball bat. A golf swing is technical in nature. You have to set aside your natural emotions or desire to swing it hard and kill the ball in favor of the technical aspect of the proper, gentle swing that uses physics and aerodynamics. This swing maximizes the way the club was built to launch the ball in the air and puts it exactly in the direction you need it to go. It's a technical process and requires the right mindset.

WHY TECHNICAL ANALYSIS IS CRITICAL FOR SUCCESS IN TRADING

Technical analysis allows us to focus strictly on price action to help put the odds in our favor.

As a trader, technical analysis offers us many advantages:

- It puts the odds in your favor for each trade.

- Technical analysis works in any time frame.

- Technical analysis works on any type of trading instrument (stocks, ETFs, options, futures, currencies, CFD's, spread betting).

- It allows you to find low risk and high profitability trade setups.

- It allows you to clearly define risk (protective stop prices).

- It allows you to forecast price several bars into the future (depending on the time frame used, could be a couple minutes or several weeks).

- Technical analysis removes the guess work from trading, allowing you to create a simple, repeatable, rule-based system in order to generate profits from the market.

- Through technical analysis, you gain clarity on market direction and risks, allowing you to focus on the important things (ignoring news & opinions). It reduces emotional stress so you can properly execute your trading strategy like a robot.

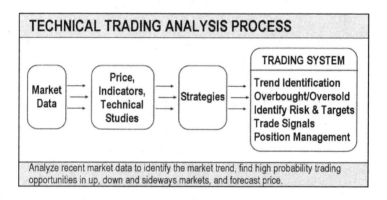

TECHNICAL TRADING ANALYSIS PROCESS

Market Data → Price, Indicators, Technical Studies → Strategies → TRADING SYSTEM: Trend Identification, Overbought/Oversold, Identify Risk & Targets, Trade Signals, Position Management

Analyze recent market data to identify the market trend, find high probability trading opportunities in up, down and sideways markets, and forecast price.

THE PROBLEM WITH TECHNICAL ANALYSIS

There are a plethora (hundreds) of 'technical analysis' indicators and tools available, and many come standard on charting websites and platforms. It is easy to get caught up in the INDICATORS and look for a "holy grail" combination so you can make your fortune trading. The issue with most traders is that they use too many indicators and tools, and they get mixed signals. Some are saying buy, and others are saying sell at the same time. Most of those indicators also LAG the market, meaning they are using data that is several bars, days or even weeks old.

So how do I know what to use and how to use it?

The good news is that I'm going to show you exactly what indicators, analysis and tools are needed and how to use them. Nothing I do is complex. Using a few specific indicators and tools, which have the least amount of lag time along with a couple which actually forecast price, gives us a huge edge in trading the market. In short, it puts the odds in our favor so the more trades we take, the more money we should make over time.

CHAPTER 4

WHAT KIND OF
TRADER ARE YOU?

There are many different trading strategies, and there are many different types of traders. Typically they can be distinguished by the time frame in which they focus on trading, whether it be investing, swing trading, momentum trading or day trading. It took me five years of painful frustration - and a lot of money - to figure out what time frame suited my personality and the lifestyle I wanted. Once I figured out what type of trader I should be, I knew where to focus my efforts. My trading became clearer, easier and more profitable. What kind of trader are you?

Every trader should step back and analyze what style of trading would work best for their current situation and lifestyle, and they should focus on learning everything they can and master it. Once you have mastered one style of trading and consistently generate profits each month, you can expand by adding more styles of trading. It is best to get one style and strategy figured out first, however, with laser-like focus. Once your brain masters one strategy and it's working for you, there will be a distinct "AHA!" moment you will experience. It is at this point that your confidence, trading and ability to create new strategies dramatically expand to new highs.

" Laser-Beam focus is mandatory for success."

"OBSESSED is a word the LAZY use to describe the DEDICATED!"

—Unknown

THE DIFFERENT STRATEGIES OF TRADING

Some people like investing, while others prefer day trading or momentum trading or swing trading. Which one are you? It's important to define who you are. You have to begin with the end in mind and know who and what you are in order to be it.

WHAT ARE YOU?

Investing: Investors enter positions because they believe in its long-term growth perspective. They have little interest in the day-to-day or even weekly price movements as they are looking to hold their positions for several years.

This is also known as the "Buy and Hold" strategy, which the media and many so called "gurus" have been saying no longer works. This subject of whether it still works or not is something that can be debated another time, but from a technical standpoint (and in my opinion), it's still a very viable method to make money over the long run. Do not let the media or other opinions make you think otherwise. If you do your research, review the long-term charts and apply basic technical analysis, you will clearly see the true answer. The problem is most of the talking heads on TV like to make bold statements in order to get more exposure and make you think you need them. They also are cherry picking the start and end dates for their wild claims, which make their opinion look and sound correct.

CHARACTERISTICS OF INVESTING

- Holding period of several years to multiple decades
- Balanced portfolio of 20 or more investments (stocks, bonds, commodities, currencies)
- Based mostly on fundamental analysis

PROS OF INVESTING

- Very passive, minimal work required

CONS OF INVESTING

- Limited to no flexibility

- Potentially large drawdowns and long periods of time with no appreciation

- Dependent on market to always move higher, with no consideration of trend

Swing Trading: Swing trading means to hold positions anywhere from five to even 30 days—and sometimes more—depending on the market conditions. Swing traders try to take advantage of certain "key" pivot points in an investment vehicles movement. For example, in an uptrend, you would buy after a pullback in price.

The saying is "Buy into Fear, Sell into Greed." I will teach you how to spot fear and greed and how to take advantage of it. Swing trading is one of the easier strategies to implement, as it works with small trading accounts and can generate very high rates of return per year. Some traders experience several hundred percent gains.

This strategy is the one I focus on the most because it provides the most opportunity with the least amount of effort. It can generate a full-time income and beyond if it is your main focus, or it can generate a steady stream of monthly income for those who have part-time or full-time jobs.

One of the big advantages of swing trading is that it can save you time. Swing traders can trade on flexible schedules. With this type of trading, you are not going to have to sit in front of your computer screen for hours at a time and stare at price charts. Instead, you will analyze the investments that you want to invest in, make the trade, place a protective stop, profit target orders and then leave. You do not have to babysit the trade and watch over it. For working individuals who are trying to integrate trading into their lives, this type of trading can be very beneficial.

This type of strategy has a few disadvantages as well. For one thing, you have to be able to let the system run its course. With this type of strategy, you have to place the trade and then walk away. Many people want to continually monitor the trade and make sure that it is doing well. The problem with this is that many traders let emotions get in the way. Instead of relying on the strategy itself, they try to intervene and usually end up making a mistake. It takes a lot of confidence in your system to look at the market, see that it is reversing against the trade that you have taken and not try to step in.

CHARACTERISTICS OF SWING TRADING

- Low drawdowns, meaning you will never take a large loss on a position. You will not be left holding positions if another flash crash or bear market takes place. Tight protective stops protect you from these things, giving you peace of mind.

- Allows you to profit in both bull and bear markets.

- Trades are few and far between, with one to four trades per month.

- Trades can be placed during market hours or for the open the next day if you have a full-time job.

- It is easy to trade and manage positions.

- It has a manageable holding period

  ○ Short-term trades are several days to weeks.

  ○ Intermediate-term trades are one to three months.

- It is a flexible, well-balanced strategy with solid reward-risk characteristics.

PROS OF SWING TRADING

- Strong risk control due to market timing through the use of technical analysis

- Flexible enough to take advantage of shorter-term technical trends in both directions

- Based on technical analysis, which works because it's based on current price action

CONS OF SWING TRADING

- Active management requires more monitoring than the buy-and-hold strategy.

Momentum/Day Trading: Trading with the intraday charts I call momentum trading or day trading. Both use the intraday price charts, and depending on the market conditions (i.e. volatility), trades can last one hour and in some cases 5 days. These trades are based on strong price movements from an intraday oversold or overbought condition, caused mainly from waves of fear or greed of market participants. But some extremes are caused by news.

This type of trading is more active, generating anywhere from one to five trades per week. I prefer and use this strategy to help generate a weekly income while my swing trades mature.

Some other benefits of Momentum/Day Trading:

- Risk per trade is low.

- Like swing trading, is a technical-based trading methodology.

- Allows you to profit from both rising and falling prices.

- Allows you capture regular 0.33% - 2.5% price fluctuations.

- Generates weekly income.

- Easy to trade and manage positions.

WHAT TYPE OF TRADER ARE YOU?

I prefer using both swing and momentum trading to get the most out of my time and the market, and to live the lifestyle I want. Keep in mind I am a full-time trader, so I have the time to watch the charts all day if I want or need to. My main focus is on swing trading the bulk of my trading account for growth. There are times when the market simply does not generate any low risk swing trading opportunities, and I have gone a few months with no trades.

The good news is that I have mastered the shorter time frame trading strategy (day/momentum trading). These trades pop up on the chart every week, giving me two huge benefits. The main one is that it satisfies my urge to trade. Why is this important? Simple. Traders naturally are addicted to being active and trading, and if your main trading strategy is not giving you any trades, you become stir crazy. You eventually search something to trade just to satisfy this urge. This leads to bad trades, and it can actually create a bad habit of straying from what you know works to a more random trading path that you really do not want to go down in most cases.

The other major benefit to knowing a second trading style is that while one may be dormant, the second strategy could be generating trades. With day/momentum trading, it can provide a weekly (or at least a monthly) stream of income to carry you through slow times.

It takes skill to refine your strategy so that it's repeatable and not rooted in emotion. No matter which one you choose, one of the most important skills that separates highly successful traders from the rest of the pack is the ability to watch the action in the market and execute trades based on what the market dictates. That's a very different perspective than simply executing based on what your internal emotion dictates. When you understand market dynamics, you can translate knowledge to profits. A well thought-out, rule-based system prevents you from impulsive decisions. When you are prepared for every scenario, you won't be tempted to react emotionally. You'll take action based on proven technical analysis and your rule-based trading strategy instead.

Technical analysis isn't just a method to analyze market action; it is a foundation to work from. It's about seeing cyclical patterns and understanding that there's an order to it amidst what might otherwise seem confusing and chaotic. Once you can understand the motivations of market patterns and anticipate what might occur next, you'll see that even though market conditions can change, there's still a cyclical movement of capital through the markets. The market is not random. There are consistent psychological motivations of humans at play, and there are consistent patterns in the market structure.

Technical analysis will help you analyze the past, all while keeping an eye to the future.

CHAPTER 5

YOUR LIFESTYLE &
THE BEST STRATEGY
FOR YOU

This section is going to provide you with insight into your beliefs in the financial markets, and it will show how you can successfully trade around and within your current lifestyle. You can focus on creating a new and more exciting lifestyle based around what you want to achieve!

At the end of this chapter there is a short assessment that will guide you to finding your optimal trading strategy, income goals and a lifestyle that fits those specific needs and goals.

If you have been lucky enough to have survived one or more major market downturns, some lessons should have been learned. For example, there always seems to be individuals that not only survive those downturns, but profit handsomely from them.

Why do certain individuals do better than others and survive bear markets? Because they have a trading philosophy that they stick to. They have strong trading strategies that they understand, and they know that while taking some risk is part of the game, a steady, disciplined approach ensures long-term success, no matter the direction of the market.

THE STRENGTH IS
IN THE STRATEGY

Your trading philosophy should be outlined before any strategies are considered. A traders philosophy is the basis for their trading policies and procedures, and ultimately their long-term plans. In a nutshell, a trading philosophy is a set of core beliefs from which all trading strategies are developed.

In order for a trading philosophy to be sound, it must be based on reasonable expectations and assumptions of how historical information can serve as a tool for proper investment guidance.

For example, the trading philosophy "to beat the market every year," while a positive expectation, is too vague. It does not incorporate sound principles. It's also important for a sound philosophy to define trade-time horizons, asset classes to use and guidance on how to respond to market volatility while adhering to your trading principles. A sound, long-term philosophy keeps successful traders on track with those guidelines rather than chasing trends and temptations.

To develop your own trading philosophy for the first time, it's important to consider covering the following areas in order to make sure your philosophy is robust:

- **Define Your Core Beliefs**

    The most basic and fundamental beliefs should be outlined regarding the reason and purpose of your trading decisions. (technical analysis based, fundamental based, 12 percent annual growth, weekly income, preferred trading instruments being stocks, options, ETF's, etc.)

- **Time Horizons**

    While traders should always plan on long-term horizons, a good philosophy should outline your unique time frame to set expectations. (Example: Focus on trades that last six to 12 weeks that play swings in the market that occur several times per year, and maybe play some quicker momentum moves in the market to generate weekly or monthly cash flow.) In short, you must know how active of a trader or investor you want to be and how long you want trades to last.

- **Risk**

    Clearly define how you accept and measure risk. The fundamental rule is the risk/reward concept: by increasing your risk, you get a potential increase in reward. (Selecting the proper trading instrument is key, as there are many to choose from, with each having their own unique level of risk/leverage built into them. I'll explain the different trading instruments in a later chapter.)

- **Asset Allocation and Diversification**

  Clearly define your core beliefs on asset allocation and diversification. Define whether they are active or passive, tightly focused or broadly diversified. This portion of your philosophy will be the driving force in developing your trading strategies and building a foundation to return to when your strategies need redefining or tweaking. (Trade individual stocks, options, ETF's, futures, a mix between them all, etc.)

THE SECRET OF SUCCESS

Successful traders limit their abilities to take large sector/investment bets outside of their core trading philosophy. While this can limit the potential upside, directional heavy weighted bets add significant volatility to your trading account.

When defining your trading strategy, it is very important to follow a strict discipline. For example, when defining a core strategy, restricting the temptation to follow or chase trends in fast-moving stocks, sectors, and commodities will keep the strategy grounded. This is not to say that one can't have additional strategies with different goals (these can be incorporated into you overall trading plan), but if you have a need or want to make these types of trades, they better be a well-planned strategy that fits into your overall core trading strategy.

OUTLINING A STRATEGY

When outlining a sound trading strategy, the following issues, which are similar to those of creating a philosophy, should be considered:

- **Time Horizon**

  A common mistake for most individual investors is that their time horizon ends when they retire. In reality, it can go well beyond retirement, and even life (if you have been saving for the next generation.) But with such a vague time horizon to pull your money out of the market to fund your retirement is a mistake. What happens if the year you retire just happens to be at the bottom of a bear market and your nest egg is down say 20, 30 or even 50 percent because you have not been planning and managing your money with your various time horizons? Your core strategy must focus on both your long-term horizon as well as your monthly or annual needs.

- **Asset Allocation**

  This is when you clearly define what your target allocation will be. Hard lines need to be drawn, and specific plans to rebalance your portfolio positions should be created when a specific position or individual strategy becomes too small or large of your portfolio and is not falling in line with your core trading strategy. Successful traders follow strict guidelines to rebalance positions. Unfortunately, most individuals often make the mistake of straying from their strategies when markets move in sharp directions. In most cases, they either start using leverage or double down on losing positions, which only compounds the issue. In most cases, it will eventually result is substantial losses.

- **Risk Vs. Return**

  At this point you should clearly define your risk tolerance. Depending on age, trading knowledge and past experiences, each individual will have their own comfort zones for how volatile their portfolio should be. With a wide array of trading instruments now available, you can now invest and trade using various levels of leverage. This is one of the most important aspects of your trading strategy since risk and return have a close relationship over long periods of time. Whether you measure it relative to a benchmark like the S&P 500, just remember to stick to your predetermined risk limits.

TRADING PSYCHOLOGY

If you've had any education in trading at all, you've heard that self-discipline is a major key to successful trading. I just want to touch on this topic for a few moments to reinforce this point! Understanding the psychology of trading is the distinction between winners and those who don't win (losers).

THE POWER OF ACCOUNTABILITY AND SELF-DISCIPLINE

Only you can be accountable for your actions. All the books, DVDs, audios, videos, manuals, courses or mentors cannot give you self-discipline. That has to come from you. That is the reason why it's called SELF-DISCIPLINE!

So what does this mean? It means understanding that to trade successfully requires an extraordinary amount of self-control and self-understanding. It requires the ability to quiet the mind when fear or greed (emotions) start to creep into your decision-making process. You must have the discipline to step back and not trade when the situation goes against your feelings. It takes the desire to delve into your psyche and to figure out what makes you do the things you do. It requires complete honesty and objectivity.

I have read a lot of trading books, and by far the most exciting ones have been about what other successful traders have done and are doing to make their fortunes. The book *Market Wizards*, by Jack Schwager, is a thorough account of trading because he interviews the world's most successful traders.

In short, his conclusion was this:

"What sets these traders apart? Most people think that winning in the market has something to do with finding the secret formula. The truth is that the common denominator among the traders I interviewed had more to do with ATTITUDE than APPROACH."

There are two aspects of trading psychology:

1. You must trust your trading method.

2. You must trust yourself.

It's obvious that to be successful in trading, you need a viable trading method with setups, rules and a plan that works. Without one, no amount of psychology is going to help you.

The technical aspect of defining a trading method is academic; the psychological power to focus and remain disciplined is much more a matter of learning the techniques of spirituality and self-improvement. Both studies may sound contradictory, but they are the yin and yang of success in just about everything. Trading is no exception.

PUTTING THE PIECES TOGETHER

It's important to remember that trading strategies define specific pieces of an overall plan. Successful traders cannot beat the market 100 percent of the time, but they can evaluate their trading results and strategies in order to reformulate their core strategy and meet or beat their goals. This could be a simple tweak, like using more capital in swing trade positions when volatility is low or decreasing position sizes during higher levels of volatility. Or you may want to add a second, third or fourth trading strategy to squeeze more trades and money out of the market.

After you have survived a few market cycles, you start to see patterns of hot or popular investment companies gathering unprecedented gains, or commodities prices rocketing higher. This was a phenomenon during the Internet technology boom. Shares of technology companies rose to rock-star levels, and investors—institutional and individual traders—lined up to buy shares. Unfortunately for some of those companies, that success was short-lived since these extraordinary gains were unjustified. Many individuals deviated from their initial core strategy in the hopes of chasing greater returns, and it ended very poorly. Individuals can model themselves after successful traders by not trying to hit home runs and instead focusing on consistent base hits. These base hits are repeated as many times as the market will provide them.

That means that trying to beat the market by long shots (large directional based trades) is not only difficult to do consistently, but it also leads to a level of volatility that will not sit well with you over the long term. Individual traders often make mistakes like shooting for the stars and using too much leverage when markets are moving up. These individuals also tend to shy away from markets as they are falling. Removing the human biases by sticking to a set approach and focusing on short-term victories is the only way to mimic the successes of winning traders.

A simple, well thought out trading strategy will likely feel slow and boring. That's because you have all the possible scenarios figured out through your strategy rules (position size, stops, profit taking levels, etc.)

"Simple = Repeatable = Boring = Mastery = Profits"

THE BOTTOM LINE

Learning from successful traders is the easiest way to avoid common errors and keep you on a focused track. Outlining a sound trading philosophy sets the stage for you, just like a strong foundation in a home. Building up from that foundation to form trading strategies creates a strong forward and upward direction; it gives you a step-by-step path to follow to your goals.

This is paramount! If you do not believe in your trading method, processes and overall strategy enough to place 10 trades in a row, knowing that some will be losers but that overall, your system has proven to be profitable, then you do not have a system with which you will be able to successfully trade. You will naturally start to second guess trade signals and not take every trade. Trading every trade that a trading strategy generates is crucial to your success. If you are losing on trades because your emotions take control, it simply means you do not have the right strategy or position size figured out to keep your emotions at bay. Technical Trading can be peaceful and profitable if you keep things simple.

SELF-ASSESSMENT ON YOUR CORE BELIEFS AND STRATEGY

Answer the questions below and make note of which ones apply to you the most. Once completed, review the

Assessment Results page to find out what your beliefs mean and how you can trade with them.

1. Do you feel stock market moves:

    1. Are Completely Manipulated

    2. Are Random & Manipulated

    3. Have Some Tradable Structure

    4. Have Some Tradable Structure &
       Some Manipulation

2. What do you feel will allow you to make profitable trades in the market?

    1. Trading based on financial news publications and the financial channel

    2. Trading based purely on fundamental data

    3. Trading based on a long term buy-and-hold strategy

    4. Trading based on fundamental data, technical analysis and position management

    5. Trading based on technical analysis, risk and position management

3. What is your preferred length of a trade that you feel fits your current lifestyle/available time?

    1. Buy and hold for years (review portfolio quarterly or never)

2. Swing Trading, playing moves which last one week to several months. (review positions nightly)

3. Momentum Trading, holding trades for 1-5 days (watching market during the days you are in a trade)

4. Day Trading, closing each position before the end of the day (watch market all session)

5. I can do day, momentum and swing trading (full-time trader)

4. Imagine you only had $100,000 to your name and it was 100 percent invested in the market. It will be pulled out of the market and given to you some time in the next 5 days, but you do not know which day. Keeping in mind that the more risk you take, the more potential profit you can gain, how much of a price swing in your account on a daily basis would make you uncomfortable? Keep in mind, your money could be pulled out of the market at any moment.

1. +/- $3,000 in value

2. +/- $4,000 in value

3. +/- $5,000 in value

4. +/- $6,000 in value

5. +/- $7,000 in value

6. +/- $8,000 in value

7. +/- $9,000 in value

ASSESSMENT RESULTS

Question 1:

- If your answer was 1 or 2, then it is best to stay away from the markets as a whole.

- If your answer was 3 or 4, then investing, trading and technical analysis is for you.

Question 2:

- If your answer was 1, 2 or 3, then you are best suited for buy-and-hold investing.

- If your answer was 4 or 5, then applying technical analysis can improve your trading results.

Question 3:

- The answer you picked that fits your current lifestyle and available time is what you should start focusing on mastering. If your answer has more than one strategy, then focusing on the strategy with the longest time frame should be your first strategy to master. Then you can start working your way down to momentum and day trading.

Question 4:

- If your answer was 1, then you should focus on trading instruments without any leverage

- If your answer was 2, 3 or 4 you can handle 2x leveraged trading instruments like ETF's and options.

- If your answer was 5, 6 or 7 you can likely handle 3x leveraged trading instruments, high-beta stocks, options and futures.

YOUR BELIEFS AND WHAT TO FOCUS ON

Now that you have a basic understanding of how you look at the markets and what you should trade, you should start to gain clarity on your long-term outlook. Focusing on the beliefs and strategies which align with your risk tolerance and lifestyle will quickly and easily bring you closer to your end goals.

One powerful quote that has proven true to me through my trading career is this one by Paul Chen.

"Passion

NEVER

Fails"

Compare your philosophy to mine!

Before you compare, remember that there are no right or wrong answers here. This is simply a gauge for you to analyze yourself. It will help you mold your trading strategies moving forward to work best for who you are, your mindset and your available time for trading.

MY PHILOSOPHY & RESULTS

The Markets Have Some Tradable Structure and Some Manipulation: I firmly believe the markets are tradable. I also know that the "big money" players can sway the market from time to time. While some despise this, I embrace it. As technical traders, we can follow the big money and ride on their coattails by using the trends and cycles they generate.

I Can Make Money Trading Based on technical analysis, risk and position management: I feel fundamental data lags the market, and it's typically in favor of the underlying market trend. Technical analysis is the key to my success. It is the basis for all my trading strategies.

I day, momentum and swing trade (full-time trader): While I may not day trade every day, I will take a trade and try to earn a few extra dollars when I see a tradable setup. But in my opinion, swing trading and playing the 1-5 day momentum shifts in the market is where a sizeable amount of money can be made.

I am comfortable with +/- $3,000 swing in my portfolio value for a $100,000 account; I don't like to see my trading account making wild swings. I understand the markets and know that anything can happen, so I keep risk well within my comfort zone. I focus on one and two base hits and never load up on any given position with excess leverage.

As for Investment vehicles, it is best if you trade what you know. I recommend learning all you can about the trading instrument that you want to focus on trading. My niche is trading the S&P 500 index by using different instruments that depend on the strategy. I focus on day trading with index futures, and when I'm in a 1-5 day momentum trade, I prefer less leverage like the 2x or 3x leveraged ETFs. For swing trades I play ETFs without any leverage, as I have the majority of my money in these positions. I will cover the investment vehicles in greater detail later in this book.

QUICK START CHECKLIST QUESTIONS TO CONSIDER FOR YOUR TRADING PLAN

If you are going to become a trader, your first step should be to develop (or follow) a checklist like this one:

- What is your goal? Define it.

- What do you need to learn and figure out to reach the goal?

- How will you measure your progress?

- How much capital is required for your strategy and desired income level?

- What type of trading best suits your personality, your available time and your goal?

- Where will you learn the about the type of trading you will be doing?

- Is there a mentor, professional trader or professional trading tool available to help speed up the process, increase accuracy and generate more profits that you should use?

- When will you begin paper trading to develop a track record and build confidence in yourself and strategy?

- What are your money management rules for maximum risk, drawdowns, position management and exit strategies?

- How will you journal all the trades in detail?

- When will you review all your trades to be sure you are on track? At the end of week or monthly?

- Be open to new ideas, indicators, tools, etc... Consider trading as a continuous learning process.

- How will you develop a trader's mentality and stay in the zone while trading?

Making this list is the first step in the right direction. The next step is to answer and clearly define everything on the list. In short, you are creating a business plan for trading. Before you start your journey, you need a map that will lead you to your destination. This is exactly what our Trading As Your Business Training Program will do. More information is listed at the back of this book.

CHAPTER 6

THE FOUR STAGES
OF THE MARKET

Markets are cyclical in nature. There is a constant process of expansion and contraction, rally and decline as the market determines the theoretical fair value of a security. The sum of these moves forms an unquestionable cyclical pattern that is consistent within all timeframes.

During a cycle, a stock enters different phases of support. It goes from irrational exuberance (typically found before its peak) to periods of widespread discontent (where its price is continually punished). However, there are never distinct good or bad stocks, indexes, etc. Every "good" investment will eventually become a bad one, and vice versa. There are, however, good trades. Good trades reward an investor who has correctly anticipated a move and positioned himself accordingly. These trades often have little to do with the underlying fundamentals of the stock market. It is these trades that are the focus of the book.

THE FOUR STAGE MODEL

Classic economic theory dissects the economic cycle into four distinct stages: Accumulation, Markup, Distribution and Decline. The concept of stage analysis was popularized by Stan Weinstein in his book, *Secrets for Profiting in Bull and Bear Markets*. A stock or index is no different; it proceeds through the following cycle:

- **Stage 1—Accumulation:** After a period of decline, a stock consolidates at a contracted price range as buyers step into the market and fight for control over the exhausted sellers. Price action is neutral; sellers exit their positions and buyers begin to accumulate.

- **Stage 2—Markup:** Upon gaining control of price movement, buyers overwhelm sellers and the price enters a period of higher highs and higher lows. A bull market begins, and the path of least resistance is higher. Traders should aggressively trade the long side, taking advantage of any pullback or dips in price.

- **Stage 3—Distribution:** After a prolonged increase in share price, the buyers now become exhausted and the sellers again move in. This period of consolidation and distribution produces neutral price action and precedes a decline in price.

- Stage 4—Decline: When the lows of Stage 3 are breached, the price enters a decline as sellers overwhelm buyers. A pattern of lower highs and lower lows emerges, and the price enters into a bear market. A well-positioned trader would be aggressively trading the short side, thus taking advantage of the often quick decline in price.

While these stages are historically defined over long time periods, they actually exist in all time frames. This allows traders to take advantage of a cycle regardless of their trading time frame. This phenomenon, known as a "fractal," exists within all investments. A fractal is simply a rough geometric shape that can be subdivided into smaller parts that have the same properties; they are a smaller version of the whole.

This is important to understand as a technical analyst because we often analyze multiple time frames. In the shorter term charts, the four stages repeat themselves many times. The combination of these short-term cycles forms a medium-term cycle, and the combination of multiple medium-term cycles forms a long-term cycle.

Recognition of these cycles is paramount in trading.

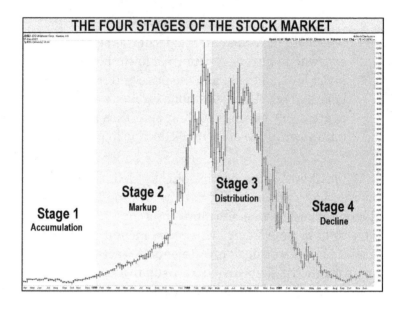

THE FOUR STAGES OF THE STOCK MARKET

Stage 1
Accumulation

Stage 2
Markup

Stage 3
Distribution

Stage 4
Decline

EMOTIONS AND CYCLICAL ANALYSIS

History has an uncanny ability to repeat itself. Whether it's the rise and fall of an empire or the rise and fall of a stock, there are clear cycles that are prevalent throughout history. People may change, but human nature and our ability to act, react and overreact is simply an innate part of our being. This predictability is what forms the basis of technical analysis, and it provides a trader with an edge. When we are analyzing cycles, we really are analyzing emotions. We are trying to gain insight as to how market participants are behaving.

Upon conducting such analysis, it can at times seem that markets are behaving "irrationally" and out of order.

Undisciplined traders often fall victim to their emotions and lose control of their objectivity. As people behave irrationally, so too does the market. Unfortunately, these conditions can persist for a long period of time. John Maynard Keynes is often quoted as suggesting that "The markets can remain irrational longer than you can stay solvent." This is a harsh reality, and it puts great emphasis on the importance of discipline, risk management and a keen eye for price action.

Emotions are what separate successful traders from those that lose money. They can be regarded as a relentless opponent, often showing up without warning and striking you at inopportune times. The successful trader is able to recognize their presence and maintain objectivity, and he is constantly assessing their own strengths and weaknesses. There will ultimately be times where you can't control your emotions, but you can always control how you respond to them.

Any time you recognize that your emotions are influencing your outlook, you are already one step ahead of the average market participant. It is at this point that you step back, refocus your perceptions, examine the price action and take the appropriate action.

An understanding of herd or mob mentality is important in trading. It can provide you with an edge over the average participant who doesn't contemplate what is happening around them.

In a mob, we never know what the feelings and motivations are of all the individual participants. There are, however, certain emotions that seem to appear at distinct times, and there is a certain predictability in their development. A stock's price action is no different. While we never know the underlying feeling and motivations of all participants, there are distinct emotions that are shared by the herd at various stages of a stock's life. An understanding of these emotions and their implications on the price action of a stock is an advantage that the profitable trader maintains.

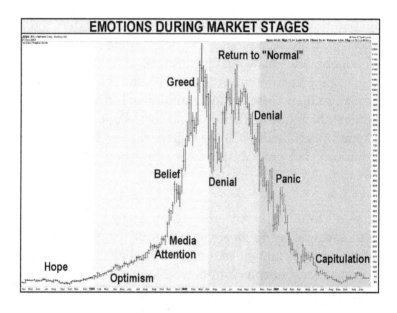

Remember, we want to keep it simple. Understanding these stages is the FOUNDATION upon which technical analysis is built. It tells you if the market is trending up, down or sideways, and each one of those market trends requires a different trading strategy to generate profits.

Focus on trading during Stage 2 Markup and Stage 4 Decline, as those are the times you will make the most money.

During sideways market conditions (Stage 1 and Stage 3), it is best to reduce your overall position sizes; trading can be more difficult during these times. With that said, if you understand inner-market analysis and cycles (which I am about to show you in a few chapters), you can make just as much money in a sideways market as you would in a trending market.

It does not matter what you trade or the time frame you trade in.

Knowing these four stages and learning how to identify them are crucial to your trading success. In my technical analysis trading course, I go into much more detail on the nuances of each stage and the best indicators and tools. But the bottom line is to understand, gain knowledge and create and utilize a proven trading system.

CHAPTER 7

SINGLE-MARKET ANALYSIS—TRADING WITH LASER BEAM FOCUS

By this stage in the game, you know that there are many investment vehicles for people to choose from to trade, like Rydex funds, mutual funds, stocks, ETFs, options, indexes, commodities, currencies and global stock markets. Many of these investments can be traded using Futures, FOREX, CFDs and Spread Betting. Once you figure out what you want to trade, you need to start researching fundamental data and technical analysis. You need to learn thousands of ways to analyze each investment. Then, to top it off, you need to select a time frame in which you want to focus on trading. Not knowing where to start focusing is ridiculously overwhelming, and it stops most traders dead in their tracks.

So let's go back to what I said early on: Keep It Simple.

While I do not have an issue with any of those options above, I do know that a trader must start somewhere. Instead of going wide (trading all kinds of things and jumping around), you should go deep and truly learn one investment really well. Stay with that type of investment until you can pull money from it on a consistent basis. Once you master one, you can start to learn another, and another, and another ... and grow over time.

TRADERS NEED TO PUT ON THEIR BLINDERS

The S&P 500 is what I love to trade. I love it for many reasons:

- Each investment has a personality of its own in terms of how it moves, how fast it moves, does it pay dividends, etc. So it only makes sense that each stock, index, bond, currency and commodity must be traded differently. With well over 8,000 stocks, hundreds of ETF's, and many index futures available, it is virtually impossible to master them all. But you need to start somewhere, and the S&P 500 has proven to be the most consistent moving investment with the most tradable price action that I have found. And the fact that it's the No. 1 traded futures contract confirms that notion.

What I like about it:

- It has consistent profitable price fluctuations on the intraday and daily charts.

- There are highly liquid investments based around it (ETFs, Options, Futures).

- Watched and traded by big money players, who provide many of the opportunities we will be trading.

- There are multiple levels of leverage available: 1x, 2x, 3x, and 50x leverage, depending on your investment vehicle.

- Pays quarterly dividends (on some vehicles).

- It's the benchmark index everyone tries to match, so why not focus on maximizing its performance!

- You can trade a large position sizes, and in many cases, all of your portfolio on this one investment (dependent on time frame in which you trade and investment vehicle used). This is a basket of 500 stocks, and it provides diversification within one simple position.

- Focusing on only one investment cuts down the noise and makes trading and position management simple.

- Allows you to drill down and analyze the INNER-Market workings (trends, cycles, volatility, volume and trader sentiment) of that individual investment for improved trading accuracy. If you know more about one investment than everyone else, do you think you can make money trading it? You sure can!

But you've got to have focus.

Early on, when I began researching about trading and technical analysis, I knew I was passionate about trading. I started soaking up all I could on the subject in college, and I even started making trades. But after I graduated, I got distracted. Getting a job so I could keep learning more about the financial markets was my main focus.

My dad and I decided to start looking for a business that was new and exciting, and one we could build and grow together. We had no idea what to do, but we decided to attend the Canton World Fair in China. There are over 40,000 products and services displayed, and we figured we could find something new and exciting there to sell in North America. After five days of intense searching for something cool, we ended up finding a handful of interesting products. We eventually narrowed down that handful to just two products. Two years later, we had our own brand name lineup of health products selling across the U.S. and Canada through our dealer network.

We grew our business from nothing to over $800,000 in annual sales by the second year, and I was finally a CEO of a corporation (this was one of my childhood dreams). We did everything, from customizing the products to be unique, ensuring they were high quality, created all the sales material, monitored the packaging, etc. It was an incredible experience, and to do it with my dad made it that much better. But after five years, we decided to sell the business and move to things that aligned more with our passions. And guess what? I still wanted to be a trader.

Focusing 100 percent on trading was my passion.

I always had inspiring, supportive parents who told me that I could do anything I wanted to when I grew up; I just had to pick a direction and go for it. I remember that after my first few trades in college, I pulled out all my money except the original $2000. I then bought what I call the BIBLE for traders. The book was called "Technical Analysis of the Financial Markets" by John Murphy. It was packed with over 500 pages of exciting insight, tools and strategies for navigating the financial markets. I studied and studied that book, and then after that I bought more books, took seminars and even hired a full-time trader to let me look over his shoulder for a few days.

That might sound extreme, but mirroring others matters. By doing this, you can learn so much and avoid making mistakes a rookie would make. Back then, I was a sponge. I soaked up everything possible about trading. I still do today because it's what I'm passionate about.

What are you currently focusing on, and what do you have to let go of in order to focus on trading? Successful trading requires laser focus. My business coach, Tony Jeary, teaches CEOs and entrepreneurs across the globe on clarity, focus and execution. Those three concepts certainly apply to Technical Trading. If you have laser focus on learning one technique and investment strategy, such as trading the S&P 500, you will be able to ignore, weed out or eliminate any emotional distractions or temptations. Don't be a master of nothing. Focus in one area and become the master.

CHAPTER 8

ONLY PRICE PAYS

A s a trader looking to pull money out of the market on a regular basis, the only thing you are really looking for is for the price of the investment you bought or sold short to move in your favor. Common sense tells us that "Only Price Pays." If the price does not move, then you do not make any money; it's that simple.

If you think it's going to help you become a better trader by reading financial articles, watching the business channel or listening to other people's opinions, you are sadly mistaken. That is the absolute best way to undermine all your hard work, analysis, training and trading. The last thing you want to be doing is second guessing yourself each time you are placing a trade or adjusting an open position.

Remember that most news and surprises follow the direction of the trend. Even if the news is against the trend, more times than not the price action will be nothing more than an intraday or one day blip on the chart. So ignore the news, rumors, opinions, tips and your emotions; be a Technical Trader!

If price movement is what pays us, then it's only logical that we focus mainly on the price. Most indicators are based off of price, so they lag the last traded price for an investment. Some indicators, like the 50-day moving average which many traders use, are actually lagging that investment by 50 days. How is a trader going to catch short-term moves in the market when they are analyzing data that is 50 days old?

Don't get me wrong, some lagging indicators work great for specific trades. I like to keep an eye on the 20-, 50-, 150- and 200-day simple moving averages. I only really like them when the investment has been trending for a long period of time and the price pulls back to the one of those moving averages. Generally you get a strong one to three day bounce off of those moving averages the first time price touches them. But the point I am trying to make here is that if you want to be more of an active trader (with daily, weekly or monthly trades to generate a steady income from the financial market), then you must focus on the things which have very little lag time and provide continuous trading opportunities. Surprisingly, if you use the proper combination of indicators, you can actually forecast short-term price movement before price moves. I'm going to show you how throughout this book.

It is very easy to get caught up in using several indicators because there are hundreds if not thousands of them. Unfortunately, many are almost duplicates of the same data shown in a different format, and many will completely contradict what other indicators are showing. This leaves you confused and frustrated, and likely trading without a clearly defined strategy.

The key to selecting the proper indicators and tools is to find what has been working best for a specific investment and the time frame in which you are trading. Using indicators that represent different types of analysis (trends, cycles, volatility, volume and market sentiment) so you do not have any overlap, you can then create a synergy of confirming indicators. They will increase your accuracy of a pending price movement in the near future.

A couple of interesting points you should know is that the stock market only trends 20-30 percent of the time. And according to J.M Hurst, the market oscillates (cycles) 20-30 percent of the time. What does this mean? It means that at best, the market provides tradable price action for us to make money only 60 percent of the time. Why is this important? It tells you that even when the market is performing well, we will still be sitting on our hands 40 percent of the time.

If you want to trade with the best odds possible, then you must have all the major bases covered in terms of analysis. Each indicator/tool that we use analyzes the market in a different way. So when several of your analysis tools are saying it's time to enter or exit a position, then you know there is a high probability of a price movement and you can take the proper course of action.

Timing Is Everything: Knowing what data to follow and analyze is a major step in the right direction, but knowing what times of the day to pull that data for analyzing is equally important. You must follow the big money players, which means you should be analyzing and trading during times when they are active.

With some instruments you can trade the financial markets run around the clock. Many traders get caught up trading the futures or FOREX market. They are still open during times when most individuals who have full-time jobs have available time, and they give those individuals at way to place some trades and satisfy their urge to trade.

But what most individuals do not know is that overnight trading is one of the toughest times to trade. Because of the lighter volume and lack of liquidity, moves can be magnified in either direction. The big money players who generate the majority of the volume and price stability during the day are out of the market.

Overnight and pre-market trading data should not be used in your analysis. For example, the S&P 500 futures contract can trade all night right into the regular trading hours. The opening bell is at 9:30 a.m. ET, and between 9:30 a.m.–9:40 a.m. (10 minutes), more contracts will be traded than what took place in the entire overnight and pre-market trading. If you trade outside of regular trading hours, be aware of the added risks involved.

With this in mind, it is important to focus on regular trading hours (9:30 a.m. ET–4:00 p.m. ET) when analyzing market data.

CHAPTER 9

INNER-MARKET
ANALYSIS

INNER-Market analysis is the study of what affects the movements of price, things like volume, cycles, volatility and market sentiment within one investment. Each of these areas provides great insight into when price should move, how far and how fast.

You can get a sense of the difference between single-price analysis and INNER-Market Analysis if you put a hand over one of your eyes and try walking around the room. With only one eye open, your field of vision is limited, and your ability to visualize your surroundings is severely restricted. Most importantly, you have no depth perception. This is how most traders make their trading decisions, with a one-dimensional view of the investment they are trading. Now drop your hand and look around the room with both eyes. You instantly can see where everything is located, and most importantly, the distances things are from you. You are really benefiting from the three-dimensional depth of the room and all its furnishings.

Go to a shooting range, and you'll observe that 99 percent of people fire their pistol or rifle with only one eye open. But those who have been highly trained often fire with both eyes open for a clear field of vision.

Don't you think you would have an advantage if you tackle your trading the same way, with both eyes wide open?

INNER-Market Analysis adds depth to your trading decisions. So as we go through these pages together, remember to keep your eyes wide open and have clear field of vision. The best traders in the world have an uncanny ability to see the unseen. And this is because they understand and use all the moving parts within a particular investment. They understand what drives the price and have created a trading strategy which keeps the odds greatly in their favor. This means more times than not, they can forecast market movements and be properly positioned prior to the move.

INNER-Market analysis gives us great insight. Don't limit yourself to single-price analysis to determine market direction. Many popular single-price based indicators are useful to one degree or another to analyze market behavior. But they are most effective when used in combination with INNER-Market Analysis to get a three-dimensional view of the market. This is not a case of "either-or." Single-price indicators should be used as a confirmation filter to INNER-Market analysis. In this manner, marginal trades can be filtered out and avoided.

This distinction can be visualized by contrasting the rectangle on the left side (representing single-price analysis) with the three-dimensional cube on the right side (representing INNER-Market analysis).

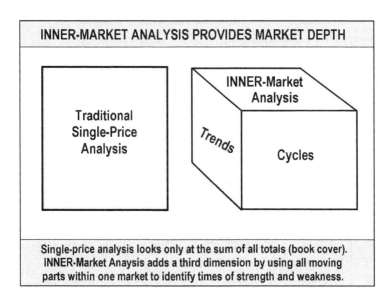

INNER-MARKET ANALYSIS PROVIDES MARKET DEPTH

Traditional Single-Price Analysis

INNER-Market Analysis

Trends

Cycles

Single-price analysis looks only at the sum of all totals (book cover). INNER-Market Anaysis adds a third dimension by using all moving parts within one market to identify times of strength and weakness.

INNER-Market analysis should be your foundation to analyze the market. It has the strengths of single-price analysis while adding another dimension to the analytic framework so that the behavior of the market can be analyzed internally as well as externally.

I have outlined some of the distinctions, from a practical trading standpoint, between INNER-Market analysis and single-price analysis in the table below:

INNER-MARKET ANALYSIS VS SINGLE-PRICE ANALYSIS	
INNER-Market Analysis & Forecasting Tool	Single Price Analysis with Lagging Indicators
➤ Identifies market strength using multiple data points	➤ Looks at one data point
➤ Is a leading indicator forecasting price direction	➤ Lags the market, causes missed opportunities
➤ Provides entry & exit points as the trend is chaning.	➤ Trades are often identified days after a trend change
➤ Protective stops, and price targets can be placed at real support and resistance levels	➤ Stop placements are often based on commonly used indicators such as trend lines, recent highs or lows
➤ False trading signals are minimized because we always know the current market trend	➤ False signals are common during sideways markets resulting in frequent losing trades
Differences between INNER-Market Analysis and Single-Price analysis highlights the importance of why it should be used.	

One mistake some traders make is not doing anything at all.

There's a fine line between action and inaction and understanding proper timing. But analysis paralysis is never good because it can get you into a cycle of waiting.

Analysis Paralysis occurs when an individual becomes so lost in the process of examining and evaluating various points of data that he or she is unable to make a decision with it! Imagine being a bullfighter paralyzed in the ring because you are unsure which way to turn. In seconds the bull takes action and charges, and if you wait then it's too late. Inaction can kill you as a bull fighter. As a trader, it means missed opportunities that can easily lead to losses in a portfolio.

Often when examining a chart to decipher which way price will move next, the pros outweigh the cons, or vice versa, and an individual has a clear direction and decision to make. When analysis paralysis sets in, it could be because the person never feels comfortable stopping his or her search for additional criteria to examine. It could be that the pros and cons are equally weighted. Or it could be a personality trait of indecision that needs to be identified and overcome because the individuals allow themselves to get stuck in a cycle of inactivity. It's like writers block or any other inactive moment that causes lockup or missed opportunity. The brain processes a plethora of information at once, and the outcome is that the human attached to the brain is locked up! Analysis paralysis is the trading version of information overload.

A trader can get overwhelmed by multiple scenarios, possibilities of movement in price action and a dozen or more indicators, and for every case there's an opposing view in the mind of the trader. The conflicting views create confusion and make it almost impossible to take action and execute trades with clarity and discipline. Impossible unless you're laser focused on clarity and discipline.

I had my fair share of analysis paralysis before I learned to keep things simple. I used to delve into all the details, putting together speculative theories that sounded great. But when it came down to pushing the button to execute a trade, I couldn't do it!

The vast information available on the internet to feed your thirst for more information is literally endless. You can search, search and search some more until you've paralyzed your mind. The dividing line between useful and necessary analysis and over-analysis is a very fine one. Whether you are a technical trader, a fundamental trader, or a combination of the two, we are all susceptible to analysis overload. Our lust for analysis cannot be satiated by the sheer amount of information available to us. But we do have a choice: We can say "enough is enough."

You probably know as well as I do how this relentless search for more information paralyzes your decision-making processes. You miss the good moves because you weren't quick enough to figure out your signal. You miss the good moves because you were otherwise engaged looking for more confirming indicators, even when you "knew" that the move was imminent. This leads to frustration.

We can easily justify the need to over-analyze, particularly with our current economic climate. We are at the beginning of a major transition from one major cycle to another. Private investors are nervous, the markets are climbing a wall of worry, and you are probably trying to analyze it all.

SO WHAT IS REALLY GOING ON HERE?

Why do we feel the need to over-analyze our analysis? Could it be that the habit is hiding a major psychological glitch? Maybe it's really a desire for control.

The need for information and confirmation fulfills a major need in all of us: the need for certainty. This need is also a primal human desire. No one likes to feel out of control, and the market can often make you feel that way because it can be uncertain and chaotic.

When the winds of change blow, the need for certainty can kick in and override the proper decision making tools that serve you as an investor or trader.

Particularly at times when we feel the wind of change blowing around us, this need for certainty becomes an overriding desire. It makes us prone to doing all those things we know will not work for us as investors and traders.

Your need to play it safe can mask a deep fear that goes right to the core of your very existence. Uncertainty makes you fear for your life. And it's like being that bullfighter staring down the bull without taking action. You have to take action and overcome the fear.

You cannot know the outcome of an event that has not yet happened. All the analysis in the world will not guarantee that you are on the right side of a trade. I know that you don't want to hear this, but your over-analysis serves as a mental safety net that cocoons you in an illusion. You think that you can predict with a higher degree of certainty the most likely outcome of an impending move in an investment.

There are only three things you can know for certain when you put on a new trade, no matter how much time you spend on your analysis:

1. You know your entry price.

2. You know where your stop is.

3. You know your position size.

Beyond that point, you are in unknown territory. Deep down, every trader and every investor knows this, even though we try to override this deep truth with the tools of our trade and the research and analysis we do every day.

Please don't get me wrong: I am not asking you to abandon your research and analysis. It is a very useful tool to give you a trading edge and should be used. However, analysis is just that: a tool and not a means to an end.

If you can become aware of the fact that your need to spend hours upon hours on analysis is actually stopping you from making money (rather than contributing to your ability to make money), you may want to look at analysis in a new way. This is what this book is hopefully helping you figure out.

You might want to ask yourself at what point your need for analysis becomes a distraction and begins to cover up other issues, like the fear of uncertainty and the need to be right.

Self-awareness and self-observation are essential skills we need to sharpen in order to become better traders and better investors.

Complex things aren't always better. For me, I think that the more simple things are, the more profound they will be. Generally traders are attracted to complex methods and systems. Complexity, however, introduces risks of over-optimization and curve-fitting. This makes systems and strategies sensitive to any change in volatility or market conditions.

Choose the methods that make sense to you and that you feel comfortable using. Choose the methods you can learn or you might already be good at. If you do this, then trading opportunities will be clear, and you will be able to effectively assess situations, evaluate risks and execute with conviction.

As Mark Zuckerberg said, "The Trick ISN'T ADDING STUFF, IT'S TAKING IT AWAY." Nothing could be more true. If you want to be a winning trader consistently, you've got to take baby steps. You need to learn one area of the market at a time and use only the best indicators and tools possible.

CHAPTER 10

IDENTIFYING TRENDS

U p until this point, we've seen how we can create calm amidst what might feel like chaos and how we can avoid pitfalls of trading by not acting out of emotion. Instead of this, we follow simple, rule-based technical strategy for trading. When you keep it simple, you avoid the complexities of overthinking. Technical Trading has many advantages.

If you think about it, there are only three directions the market can move. In financial lingo, a bull market is an uptrend, a bear market is a downtrend and consolidation is a sideways trend. Each of these trend types requires a different trading strategy in order to pull profits from the market consistently.

CHARACTERISTICS OF TRENDS

Uptrends are a series of price advances followed by price declines which do not violate the prior low (higher highs and higher lows). During an uptrend, the prior low will act as a support level while the prior high will act as resistance. It is important to remember that when an investment is trending in a direction, the odds favor a continuation of the trend rather than a reversal. Knowing this, it is only logical that the best position during an uptrend is a long trade.

All trends eventually come to an end, so after the price has risen, it will eventually begin to weaken and struggle to make new highs. This is when a sideways trend (consolidation) develops.

Sideways trends are a series of highs and lows that are approximately at the same level. The highs mark resistance, and the low serve as support. This trend is also referred to as a range-bound market, as price is stuck in a sideways range, bouncing between support and resistance.

After a long sideways trend, the price of the security will often reverse the prior direction. In this case, the prior trend was up, so it will fall in to a downtrend.

Downtrends are a series of price declines followed by price advances that do not violate the prior high (lower lows and lower highs). The prior high will act as resistance, and the prior low will serve as support level.

Here is a simple visual of the trends:

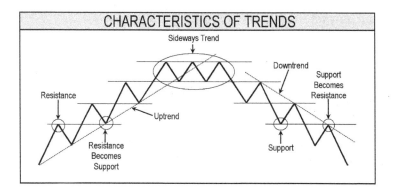

I am sure you have heard this saying before, but it cannot be overstated. The biggest problem traders have is trying to outthink the market by trying to pick a top or a bottom. Trends are more likely to continue than they are to reverse, and trends can last much longer than you think. Depending on the time frame in which you are watching the market, a trend can last for years. In some cases it can even last when all economic data, news and market sentiment is opposing. There is no reason to bet against it.

Trade With The Trend—The Trend Is Your Friend!

TREND IDENTIFICATION
PART I—MOVING AVERAGES

Moving averages are the most commonly used indicator, and they therefore provide significant information about the market in a simple to understand format.

Moving averages have multiple functions serving as support and resistance levels depending if the price is trading above of or below it.

A moving average tells you the average price over the chosen time period and length. For example, the 20 Simple Moving Average, which is my favorite, shows you the average price of the last 20 data points. So if my focus is on the daily chart, then the 20 SMA would show me the average price of the last 20 days.

I use various moving averages in my strategies and trade setups, and these are the ones I watch very closely for support or resistance levels: 20, 50, 150 and 200 simple moving averages.

The following chart shows these moving averages:

DIFFERENT TYPES OF MOVING AVERAGES:

- Simple Moving Average (SMA).

- Exponential Moving Average (EMA) gives more weighting to the recent data points to help reduce lag time.

- Weighted Moving Average (WMA) uses a system giving even more weight to the recent price action to help reduce lag time and predict trend reversals sooner.

The moving averages (MA's) that are most widely used are the simple moving averages. All the MA's I refer to and use are simple moving averages.

TRADING WITH THE MOVING AVERAGE

Recognizing the direction of the trend will be crucial to your success. I often reflect on a basic concept that was taught to me when I first began trading: news, stock fundamentals and most technical indicators are all going to be affected by the direction of bigger market trends in play.

The market is a discounting mechanism, meaning it typically reverses direction months—and in some cases up to a year—before the underlying economic data and news changes from good to bad, or vice-versa. I found that concept difficult to accept at first, but over time it has proven itself year after year.

Moving averages are an effective smoothing filter of the overall price trend, AND they provide a great early warning to a changing trend. By combining a smoothed average with cycle analysis (which I talk about in the next chapter), we can get a clear perspective of the overall market health. The synergy that both trend and cycle analysis creates will give you with the confidence to help you remain on the right side of the market.

A general rule for trading the S&P 500 index: When the 20 SMA is pointing up, we can hold long positions in the market. When price dips to the 20 SMA, we can use that to add to our long positions. Going the other way, when the average is pointing down, it is time to exit long positions. We should short the market, using each rally back to the 20 SMA as a short entry point.

20 Simple Moving Average Trend Trading

TREND IDENTIFICATION
PART 2—CYCLES

I'm sure you have heard the saying that a rising tide lifts all boats.

Well, think about a rising or falling tide and what it does. Dinghies and yachts are equally affected by the up and down motion of a tide.

Similarly, both weak and strong stocks are greatly influenced by the rise and fall of the broad market.

After all, the market is the sum of all stock action. The interesting thing here is that most stocks, like boats in a tide, tend to move in a synchronized motion. This is regardless of the valuation or news surrounding each individual stock.

If on any given trading day a stock's price could move up or move down, and the direction was random, we would see on average, half of all stocks rise up and the other half move down. This would lead to the broad market being flat or not moving up or down. But the reality is, on any given day, a majority of stocks will moving in the same direction. This tells us that there is a directional influence and that not all movement is random for individual stocks.

The forces which move the financial markets are not as vague as you may think. A large part of market direction is the effect of regular cyclic forces in play. These cycles are much like waves in the ocean, where the rhythmic motion of the water forms a series of peaks and troughs.

Cycles can be identified and measured over time, but their length and height (amplitude) will change slightly from time to time. These cyclical patterns in the financial markets are created from a variety of recurring economic conditions, calendar events and human behavior. What is exciting about this is that these periodic cycles continue to reappear over time with a high degree of predictability.

For the trained investor, these seemingly random explosive moves in the market are actually predictable. They tend to occur when multiple cycles from multiple time frames converge, forming a significant low or high at the same time. This increases the probability of price-reversing direction and has with a lot of power behind it. The combined force of each creates an enormous move that takes most untrained market participants by surprise.

Some individuals refer to the waves in the market in terms of fear and greed, or they say that prices become either overbought or oversold for the time frame in which the main cycle appears on. I don't think there is a right or wrong answer, but I do think it is a little more complex than that. As we will discuss later, many of the cyclic influences are derived from calendar-based events. While other cyclic influences are more unclear in terms of why they exist, they are reliable in the fact that they do appear regularly on the chart.

Unfortunately, being the emotional creatures that humans are, we tend to be influenced by almost every distraction the market throws our way. The news often blurs the bigger picture, causing us to try and pick a market top or bottom. When we react emotionally to the news or a quick change in market price, we often act against our own best interest. How many times have you traded on breaking news and sudden price movement only to have the position you just entered quickly reverse?

It takes self-discipline to step back and remain focused when so much of the daily noise distracts us. Many traders become so fixed in a position that they fail to recognize a market changing its trend right before their eyes. Many traders will stand firm and try to wait until they are right, but many times that doesn't happen and significant losses can be incurred.

In order to become successful in trading, we need to become less attached to favorite trends or positions. While some of us like to only trade long positions and others like to short, the more skilled we become at reading the market, managing our money and knowing when, where, how much and for how long our next trade should last, the more it becomes a habit that does not require much effort. The issue is not whether the markets are going to move up or down because we can figure that out through our analysis. Success requires that we observe and follow the market's trend with a plan and readiness to act. Not being prepared and ready to trade leads to hindsight of lost opportunities and to possible financial loss.

THE ONLY LEADING STOCK MARKET INDICATOR THAT WORKS

It drives me crazy when I hear people say you can't predict the markets. If that were true, no one would make a consistent profit, and no one would choose a career as a trader. That's like a professional golfer saying you can't predict which way the wind will blow the ball. You can't control the wind, but you are able to monitor it and understand how to utilize the direction of it.

Financial institutions wouldn't employ rooms full of well-paid analysts to read the charts and crunch numbers all day long if it were true that you cannot predict the stock market. The truth is, big money players treat what they know like a game of poker.

They bluff and fake out other market participants by manipulating and pushing prices beyond short-term support and resistance levels, and they get you to take the other side of the position they want. They do not want you to know where the market is going to move next, and by playing these market manipulation games, they are able to make consistent gains while others lose.

The good news is that they can't hide what they are doing from a well-educated, focused and fully armed technical trader. We uncover big money activity brewing below the surface. And a technical trader anticipates their moves rather than explaining in hindsight what key turning points are developing and where institutional money is flowing. That's critical information you need to know before putting your money to work in the market.

You will not see these kinds of forecasting results anywhere else. We are able to identify momentum cycles in the market, which last 1-5 days in length, and also larger swing cycles, which last 1-12 weeks in length. This shows you where institutional money is going and how long a particular trend will last.

You've likely already experienced institutional trading at work and not have even known it. They do the majority of their buying during market "dips," or times when lower prices occur and minor support levels have been broken. One common strategy the institutions use is "running the stops." They run the stops by spooking the majority of traders out of the market just before price reverses and rallies. This happens on a regular basis and during both up and down trends.

Alternatively, if you look back on the price charts, take note of how rallies fail to make new highs—above previous highs—during a down trend. Those rallies failed because institutional traders use each successive bounce in price to sell into the strength. This means they can exit any remaining long positions or enter new short positions in preparation for the next sell off in stock prices.

In 2001 a fellow trader got me interested in stock-market cycles, and at that time there were only a few others trying to figure out how best to identify, apply and trade using that information. It took me by surprise, but after researching, analyzing and building tools based around cycles, it was clear that cycles in the stock market were real and surprisingly consistent!

In that moment, I knew it was time to learn everything I could on stock market cycles so I could improve my market timing. I wanted to be able to forecast turning points and lengths of new trends. Cycles have improved our timing for entry, profit taking and exit, which obviously helps boost our trading profits and return on investments significantly.

WHAT CREATES STOCK MARKET CYCLES?

Just like waves in the ocean, stock markets create complex wave patterns. Market movement is actually a summed total of the individual oscillations from its component stocks. A good example of this is similar to what surfers see when they are out surfing. On any given day, the ocean is creating several different sizes of waves. But every few minutes, several of the various waves happen to be moving together. This synergy of waves moving as one generates what is called in surfer terms as a "set." When multiple waves move together as one, they carry more power (amplitude/height). These "sets" take place every day, and they are the most wanted waves to ride. On a calm day, these sets may only be a foot high, but during big storms (high volatility market times) they can create huge waves.

Interestingly, individual stocks have several waves of oscillation within their own price movement. These are waves within waves. Let's consider some of the reasons why those exist.

The flow and periodic price motion for any given stock or stock market can be caused by a few things:

- **Economic Data** can cause large waves of money to flow in our out of stocks, sectors or indexes as a whole.

- **Quarterly earnings** reports can affect the perception of a stock's potential going forward and can trigger a wave of buying or selling from the anticipation or release of the results.

- **Seasonal sales** cause an increased interest in the sector or stock. This is frequently seen in the retail sector before or after holidays.

- **Stock options** expirations occur on a regular basis, and they are used by traders to hedge positions that cause extra buying or selling after expiration.

- **Bi-monthly fund contributions** are funds whose members deposit money with each paycheck.

- **Herd/Mob psychology known as Market Sentiment**
  Traders move in sync—like a school of fish—when
  extreme fear or greed is surging through their veins.

There are other factors that can affect a stock's price, and
we may not always be aware of every underlying "reason"
for them.

The Key To Cycle Analysis: It's not "why" cycles move the
way they do that is critical; rather, it's knowing the direction
and the size of each developing wave that tells you ALL you
need to know to start earning big profits and to properly
protect yourself against reversals.

Stock Market Cycles:

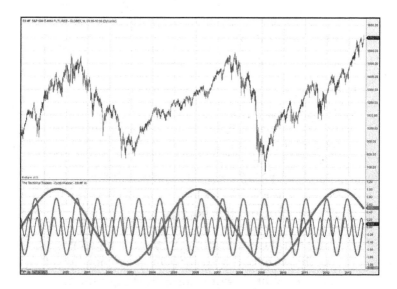

The same theory and cyclical factors for individual stocks can be applied to the stock market as a whole; this will dramatically improve your market timing and profits. Remember, fear is the most powerful force in the stock market. So when analyzing cycles, be sure to focus on matching cycle lows with price lows.

In order to identify the most active cycles and their direction, speed and frequency within a market, commodity, currency or an individual stock, you'll need a spectra tool. Armed with this financial information, we can know with confidence whether it's time get off the train or whether it's time to get on for a ride.

Fortunately, some very brilliant mathematicians and engineers figured out how to develop such tools. Over the years I have developed and improved the process of learning how to identify and apply active cycles to the financial markets. This tool filters complex and noisy stock-market data, and it separates the underlying periodic wavelengths (cycles) within the data.

When we apply that knowledge to the market index, we can see the data arranged in waves and we can see which wave lengths have the most or least power behind them. This method of analysis allows us to instantly identify the important waves. These waves move prices for virtually any type of investment, such as individual stocks, sectors, indexes, commodities, silver, gold, crude oil, currencies, etc.

CYCLE LENGTHS TO FOCUS ON

Investing Cycle The investing cycle is the longest cycle we follow. It ranges between 11 to 14 years from trough to trough. While its trend is very powerful, it is much harder to invest or trade than you may think. The price and, more importantly, the percent swings are huge and much more than most traders can handle. The market will fluctuate at times over 30 percent against the current trend during a simple correction. This cycle is not one I trade because we can actively play these individual 30 percent rallies/ correction using a shorter-term cycle and make a lot more money.

The investing cycle also has the largest amplitude of all the cycles we follow. When this cycle is moving up and when the shorter-term cycles are also moving upwards, its directional force will provide extra lift in the market. When the shorter cycles are moving down against the investing cycle, price may only correct briefly or pause (trade sideways) until the shorter term cycles are clearly heading back up.

Remember, cycles are more of a forecasting tool that gives you advanced warning of a trend reversal. So do not jump the gun and try to outthink the cycles by getting into position early. You really do need to see the cycles moving in you favor, along with price, before getting on board with the trend.

Swing Cycle, which I consider to be the most profitable trading cycle in the stock market, has a cycle length of about –three to six months. You will often hear this cycle referred to as the current trend. If this cycle is rising, then the trend is up; if it's falling then the trend is down. We then time our trades with the next shorter cycle, called the momentum cycle, to trade in favor of the current trend (swing cycle).

Here is what that can look like:

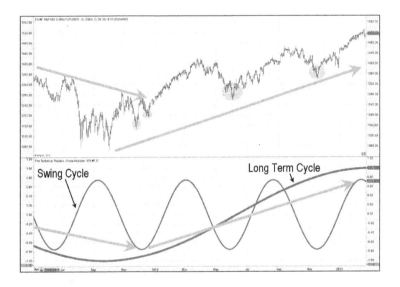

When we make decisions about trading, we want to consider the time frame for each of our investments. If we are a day trader or momentum trader, we certainly want to make sure that our trades are with the direction of the current swing cycle. Trying to trade against this trend is like swimming upstream; profits will tend to be small, and a lot of extra work is required. This is referred to a counter-trend trade and should only be done by experienced traders.

The Swing Cycle is the foundation of my analysis. It identifies the current market trend, and it is also what my core trading strategy was built to trade from. This cycle clearly helps determine the best direction (long or short) for trades. Focusing on long positions during an uptrend (trading with the trend and buying during swing cycle bottoms) is the most profitable play while this cycle is rising. Taking shorter positions (counter-trend trades) is more risky and must be actively managed for small, quick profits. Shorting the market when the swing cycle is trending down will yield the most profitable positions (short selling during swing cycle tops). Remember that prices tend to fall three to seven times faster than they rise. So when shorting the market, be ready for fast moves, and be ready to take profits off the table.

Three or four times each year, the Swing Cycle will bottom. When that occurs, it represents an exceptional buying opportunity in which markets will typically rally 5 percent to 15 percent in the following months. During these times there will be multiple entry points that you can find by using other technical indicators, along with the momentum cycle bottoms. These will get you properly positioned.

Momentum Cycle has a length of about one to five days. This is the shortest cycle I trade, and it allows for quick profits each week. The moves have enough momentum behind them that even if you have a bad entry or exit point (and sometimes both), you can still make some money. While the Swing Cycle indicates the current trend and future price direction, the Momentum Cycle uses a combination of direction, speed, volatility, volume and market sentiment.

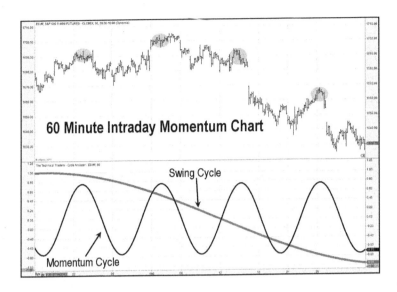

60 Minute Intraday Momentum Chart

Swing Cycle

Momentum Cycle

A simple use for the Momentum Cycle is to wait for instances when it has bottomed and turned back up. Only then should you be looking to enter long positions. The opposite is true during a down Swing Cycle, as you want your shorter term trades to be in favor with the next longer cycle. Only look to enter short positions or to buy inverse exchange traded funds (ETF's) once the cycle has topped and is starting to move back down. Remember cycles forecast the price in advance, so if you try to front run (i.e., get in early before cycle tops/bottoms) your timing will likely be poor. This can result in losing trades. Keep in mind, some of the strongest moves in the market take place just before a trend reverses. Do not try entering earlier, or it may be costly.

The bottom line is that we can see where cycles will be in the coming days or weeks. And by adding a few confirming indicators through the use of technical analysis, we can position our trades to profit from the next market move!

UNDERSTANDING CYCLE SKEW IN THE STOCK MARKET

As a trader or investor, our task of predicting and timing the stock market would be much simpler if cycles were perfectly formed like a sine wave and never changed their frequency or amplitude. But we know that over time, they gradually change. Depending on whether stocks are in a bull or bear market, their peaks will skew right or left. And during a strong trend, they can become flattened or dampened.

If you look at real example of active cycles in the S&P 500 index, you will see how they interact with each other. They allow us to time our trades and forecast into the near future where the price should be trading, and it allows us do this with a high degree of accuracy.

In the chart below, you will see three individual cycles located at the bottom. The middle section of the chart is the three cycles "combined" as one. This shows how each cycle affects the overall trend strength. The longer term cycle always plays a role in supporting or subtracting from the next shorter cycle strength (amplitude).

Located at the top of the chart is the S&P 500 index. Take note of how it closely represents the summed total of these cycles. The shorter term cycles add or subtract from that of the longest cycle trend. Diverging cycle movement in the market is called a "counter trend."

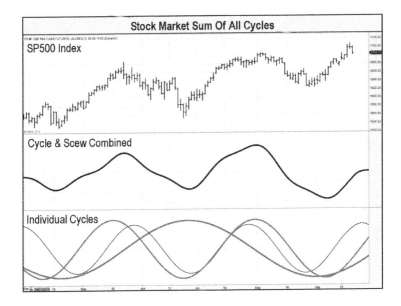

Stock Market Sum Of All Cycles

SP500 Index

Cycle & Scew Combined

Individual Cycles

UNDERSTANDING CYCLE DAMPING IN THE STOCK MARKET

The longer the cycle length, the stronger its influence. But when multiple cycles are forming tops and bottoms at different times, the market can get choppy and volatile. This is typical during a transition period in the market, and it is similar to Stage 1 and Stage 3 in the market life cycle. This occurs before a trend changes. During these times, strong waves of buyers and sellers flood the market. This can be seen through increased volume and volatility levels.

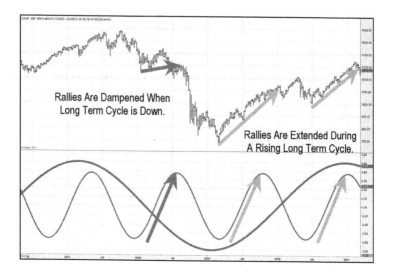

In the chart above, notice the long-term cycle (blue line) is trending down. In a down trend, shorter term cycles, including price, are "damped" or compressed. When the shorter term cycle is trending up, price only moves up a little, or it only trades sideways. The longer term cycle has a negative effect on price.

Now, compare the price when the blue and green cycles move with a rising, longer term cycle. Pullbacks are shallow, and rallies are extended.

This is why we focus on trading with the trend. We avoid "counter-trend" cycles as short trades, though when a pullback is likely to start, it is wise to lock in some profits as part of your trading strategy. If anything, during a trending period, we'll use counter-trend moves as a method to time our entry or re-entry into the current trend.

This is why we say, "Don't trade against the Swing Cycle." The Swing Cycle is one of the most cyclically active components in the market, and it can last from four to 12 weeks in its trending phase.

While cycle analysis is very powerful, it still requires additional analysis and position management. This is to be sure you enter and exit the market at optimal times with the most profits possible.

The only thing that will affect the swing cycle's strength is the direction of the long-term cycle. When both are moving in the same direction, be prepared for some very strong market moves. When opposing each other, look for extended periods of a sideways and choppy market.

HOW TO FORECAST WITH CYCLES

To this point in our discussion, we have been examining trends and cyclical influences on the market. We are now going to talk about how to increase the likelihood of our investing/trading success by forecasting the stock market's behavior. A benefit to understanding cycles and other trending influences is that they have a measurable length of time. We can, with a great degree of confidence, project them into the near future to give us a clearer picture of where are markets are headed. They will tell us if we should expect more of a trending or choppy market.

The market whole is greater than the sum of its parts. The stock market is the sum of its parts: all sectors, stocks, fundamentals, investor/trader emotion and their resulting behavior. Our effort will be focused on the summed total market picture. That uses both cycles and complimentary technical analysis tools, and it creates a powerful synergy that will impact your trading and positions more than almost anything else you could study.

Through the use of different timeframes, you will begin to see that the markets are factual. This means there are many identical yet smaller price patterns occurring inside of larger trends. Our perspective will be formed by stepping back and separating the bigger picture of bull and bear market cycles. We then focus on the swing and momentum cyclical moves (often described as overbought or oversold conditions) that can be profitably traded up and down within the bigger trend.

Several upside trades can last for months and frequently occur within a major bear market, just as many downside trades can be very profitably traded during a raging bull market. Once you begin to understand the regularity of both types of opportunities, you will not be so easily panicked by the chatter and second guessing that comes from financial talking heads and so called experts.

TURNING CYCLES INTO PROFITS

It was not many years ago that stock-market forecasting seemed unscientific. Technology has also changed the way we extract information from the markets. With so much fundamental, technical and individual opinions available to anyone with an internet connection, too much of what we digest is a rehash of the type of analysis that was used before we had high quality charting platforms. They are based on single-price analysis versus the more in-depth cycle and sentiment analysis we are able to use today. With our unique thinking and readily available technology, however, we are able to trade and forecast price to a whole new level if done correctly.

As a technical trader, you will be able to take advantage of some improvements that were not available until recently. It can provide you with valuable insight into current cycle behavior, and it can help you better plan your positions entries and exits.

Whether you are trading long or short positions, cycle analysis identifies key turning points before a trend change is likely to occur. The strength of our cycle analysis is in its ability to identify those turning points without the lag effect found in most technical indicators.

WHAT ARE THE KEY BENEFITS TO USING CYCLE ANALYSIS?

Cycles are the one indicator that allows us to predict the direction of the stock market.

1. It tells you which direction the market is trending.

2. It shows us when a change in the trend is about to take place, allowing us to take profits and prepare to change strategies.

3. It identifies pullbacks or bounces, which we can
   use to lock in gains or re-enter a trend.

4. It alerts us to price swings before they happen.

Cycle analysis is unlike anything you have ever used,
and when applied to complimentary technical indicators
and trade management, you have a very complete, simple
and profitable trading strategy for all market conditions.

It will be difficult at times to ignore the voices and
opinions of others in the market place. But if history has
proved anything, we know most of the news and daily
opinions are generally counterproductive to our trading.
Learning cycles, complementary technical analysis tools
and following your own proven trading strategy will lead
to more profit than almost any other market research you
can pursue.

Cycle analysis will become an invaluable tool to your
trading strategy and long-term success as a trader. Having
this information gives you an edge on knowing when those
key turning points are developing in the markets, and
better yet, it tells you how to manage your positions and
anticipate your next trade.

CHAPTER 11

VOLATILITY IS YOUR FRIEND

How do you view volatility? Some people look at volatility as their enemy. To many traders, an increase in volatility means large percentage moves that are fast moving and random in nature. Yes, it is true that price movements are faster than normal, and it is true the size of the prices swings increase. But price movements moving at random could not be further from the truth.

I view volatility as an adventure similar to that of a roller coaster. When you are standing in line for a roller coaster, what you see and feel? As you stand there looking up as the massive hills and loops which you are about to experience, you know that things will be crazy and exciting during the ride. This is similar to how I look at volatility. An increase in volatility simply means price is going to start moving up and down at a faster pace than what you are likely comfortable with. Remember how I talked about how market participants move like a school of fish during times of extreme fear and greed? Well, just like a roller coaster doing a loop-to-loop, there will be people screaming in fear while others are yelling with excitement.

I call fear the most powerful force on the planet. When true fear sets in, human behavior becomes predictable, and investors and traders will move as a group. This means price movement is not random, and it therefore can be traded more accurately. During times of fear, positions are sold by the majority of market participants at an accelerated speed and with a lot of force behind it (volume). These moves are what create rising volatility levels, and spotting opportunities in the market during times like this can generate huge profits in a very short period of time. So I ask you the question:

Are you going scream and panic out of your positions, or will you be a trader with a trading strategy that identifies these situations? A trading strategy allows you to see them as an opportunity to generate profits while others trade emotionally.

Volatility is your friend. If you understand it, accept it, adapt to it and harness it, you'll grow to love volatility and utilize it to your benefit.

HOW VOLATILITY AFFECTS PRICE

Volatility refers to the amount of uncertainty, or price movement risk, in a security's value. A higher volatility means that a security's value can potentially trade in a larger price range. This means that price can change dramatically over a short time period in either direction. On the flip side, a low volatility means that a security's value will not fluctuate as dramatically, and it means that it will change in value at a steady pace over a period of time.

THE FEAR INDEX

The index we use to gauge the strength of near term price movements, along with market participants' level of fear or greed, is the CBOE volatility index. This is also known as the VIX or the FEAR INDEX.

While trading with fear is the absolute worst thing anyone can do, trading when others are fearful can be very rewarding. Technical traders with a proven method of analysis and trading strategy are lucky; they understand the potential risks involved for each trade and for each market condition. Knowing what could happen and knowing the odds of an impending move greatly reduces the level of fear one may encounter.

Simply put, a fearful trader will break down and fall victim to trading off their emotions. They will chase prices higher, and they will sell positions after they have already sold off, only to see the security reverse shortly after. You should know by now that the market thrives off emotional traders. The market chews them up and spits them out day after day. If you show any level of emotion in your trading, the market will come after your money. And once you've lose most of your money, it will try to take yourself confidence and pride. The market has no mercy.

The good news is that we can measure the level of fear in the financial market through the CBOE Volatility Index chart. Using this, we can anticipate the size of the next market move and its direction. The ticker symbol is VIX, and it shows the market's expected level of volatility looking forward 30 days. It's constructed using the implied volatilities of a wide range of S&P 500 index options. This volatility is forward looking, and it is calculated from both put and call options.

I am going to briefly touch on how I deal with fear and greed as emotional drivers for my trading so you can see how they affect me. I'm a guy who likes rules and processes because they make life, tasks and trading easier. So when the market generates a trade or a position adjustment, the fear or greed that drives my trading is the fear of not executing the trades perfectly to what my system requires. I'm not perfect by any means; we are human, and humans make mistakes. It's easy to think you are doing the right thing, but without a step-by-step guide for each trade or adjustment, I still enter the wrong order type, protective stop or target price. As mentioned earlier in the book, setting goals based on focusing on the process is how I use fear. My fear is based about making sure my execution is following my process, and as long as I do that, my end goal of making money naturally occurs.

As much as I would love to remove my own fear and greed from the equation, it is impossible. We will always have our own opinion or feeling of what the market will do next no matter what our technically proven system is telling us to do. While I think I manage my emotions well, I know that my heart is still pounding in my chest with either fear or greed during times when my system is flashing a new trade or position adjustment. I have to bite my lip at times, enter the trade and make the leap of faith that my system has my best interest in mind. After all, it has proven time and time again that I should follow its rules. With that being said, when a trade does play out in my favor—which they do over 80 percent of the time—the feeling that I experience is truly amazing. I feel like I am on top of the world with excitement and confidence, and I am overwhelmed with a feeling of accomplishment. You won't feel these things without having a plan and having the courage to execute it.

There are three variations of volatility indexes: the VIX tracks the S&P 500, the VXN tracks the NASDAQ 100, and the VXD tracks the Dow Jones Industrial Average.

THE MOST ACCURATE VOLATILITY INDEX

The S&P 500 Volatility Index (VIX) is what we focus on to track current market volatility levels in our trading analysis. We have found this index to provide the most timely and accurate insight for gauging the level of fear in the market. This index has the largest basket of stocks, which provides a diversification of sectors for an accurate snapshot of market sentiment.

VIX values above 30 are generally associated with a large amount of volatility; this means daily price fluctuations are much larger than normal. A value below 20 indicates low levels of fear in the market. Price will trade in a more condensed price range, and it carries less risk for investors.

THE SECOND MEASURE OF VOLATILITY— STANDARD DEVIATION

Standard deviation is a statistical term. It measures the amount of variability or dispersion around a security's average price. Standard deviation is also a measure of volatility. Dispersion is the difference between the actual value and the average value. The larger the dispersion or variability is, the higher the standard deviation. And the smaller this dispersion or variability is, the lower the standard deviation. As technical analysts, we can use standard deviation to measure expected risk and determine the significance of certain price movements. We do this by using a classic distribution bell curve.

Even though a security's price may not always be normally distributed, technical analysts can still use the normal distribution guidelines to gauge the significance of a price movement. In a normal distribution, 68 percent of the price action falls within one standard deviation, 95 percent of the price fluctuations fall within two standard deviations, and 99.7 percent of the time price will be within three standard deviations. Using these stats, we can improve our market timing, knowing with a high degree of certainty that price should reverse direction to the average once these levels have been reached.

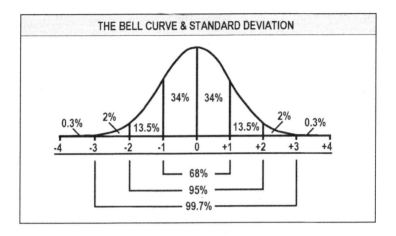

It only makes sense that when the market volatility is rising or falling, the standard deviations value range will also be expanding and contracting. Using both volatility and standard deviation together will paint a clear picture of near term price support and resistance (oversold and overbought) levels on the price chart. It also will show how quickly price is expected to move.

THE HYBRID INDICATOR: VOLATILITY + STANDARD DEVIATIONS

This is an indicator I developed, and I use it often as a tool for timing entries, profit taking, and exiting positions when there is a change in trend. This tool generates overbought and oversold arrows on the chart. It is based on the current volatility level and specific standard deviation criteria for the S&P 500 index. The results you get when combining volatility and standard deviations are astounding.

Think of the stock market or a stock's price as if it were a guitar string. If you were to strum lightly on the string, it would vibrate quietly and in a narrow range. Now, if you were to pull the string with two fingers really hard and let go, you would get a much larger vibration range (high volatility). We know the farther is it pulled in one direction, the higher the chances are that it will be released and return to the norm. A string or price of a stock can only be pulled so far in one direction before its reverses in most cases. But strings can break and stock prices can collapse, and because of this, we must have protective stop orders in place.

When price surges or dips beyond specific standard deviation levels, the odds favor a reversal in price back to the average. This allows us to forecast an imminent trend change. With that being said, it is crucial that you always trade in the direction of the longer and underlying trend. For example, you would only focus on buying the dips with green arrows, locking in partial profits and tightening your protective stop once a red overbought arrow has been reached during an up trending market.

Essentially we what we are doing is watching for securities to be pulled down or pushed up to extreme levels that we know are not sustainable in the current market environment. Then we enter a position and expect the security to move back within its normal trading range.

DAILY CHART HYBRID INDICATOR TOOL

Below is the daily chart showing how by using only volatility, you can catch one to two percent price moves on a regular basis while building a long position.

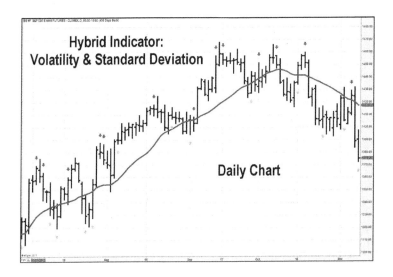

INTRADAY CHART HYBRID INDICATOR TOOL

Volatility analysis works in all time frames, as you can see from the 30-minute intraday chart below. The only differences between the two time frames of daily charts and intraday is the fact that price movements happen in a shorter period of time and with a smaller percentage of potential gain. You can see these wild intraday movements in the market, which send most individuals into a panic, can be the perfect trading opportunity for those who know what to look for! Volatility is your friend.

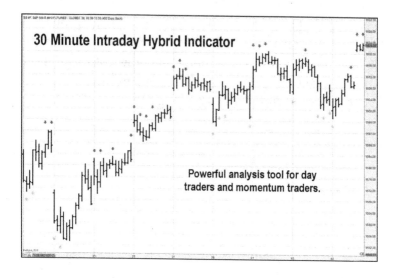

30 Minute Intraday Hybrid Indicator

Powerful analysis tool for day traders and momentum traders.

These extreme price levels provide technical analysts with valuable insight for where price is expected to move in the near future. This hybrid volatility and standard deviation indicator automatically adjusts with the market. The constant expansion and contraction in price and volatility no longer becomes a process to calculate manually. When price reaches an extreme level (one that is deemed significant enough to warrant your attention for a trade), the chart generates a trade arrow. This tool should be used in conjunction with trend and cycle analysis to improve your market timing accuracy even more.

How much information is enough? You're reading this book to gain knowledge and sharpen your skill set. By increasing your knowledge, you're able to evaluate market conditions and trading strategies in advance. To succeed in the financial markets, you can't treat your trading as if it's a hobby. You are either taking other people's money, or they are taking yours!

Treat it like a business, and invest your time and energy into understanding all facets of the financial market. You'll have to spend time and money to succeed, just as you would in anything else that's important to you. And most importantly, don't give up! Research, learn, apply and grow.

PASSION NEVER FAILS!

CHAPTER 12

VOLUME = POWER = SENTIMENT

E ach form of analysis we have covered used a specific indicator or tool, allowing us to use that information. Each plays a critical role in helping identify the market trend, the current cycles in play, and extreme volatility swings for imminent price reversals. Volume plays an equally important role in order for us to understand price.

While most individuals look at volume in terms of how much power/commitment is behind a price movement when reviewing chart patterns, I look at volume a little differently.

I read volume as a gauge for market psychology, as it can tell you what is going on in the emotional psyche of buyers and sellers. Volume and price have a symbiotic relationship, and experienced traders understand how to analyze and interpret them together.

Volume is the best indicator of how emotionally invested individuals are at any specific moment. For instance, high volume may indicate emotional commitment or mania, while low volume may indicate complacency or apathy, or nothing at all. Understanding the movements of the market as it relates to volume can help you significantly. I will show you how in this chapter.

It is important to know that when you are analyzing volume by using basic technical analysis rules for reading chart patterns, volume shouldn't be used as a timing indicator. Don't wait to see volume before you buy, or you might miss out on the next move altogether. Unlike my unique NYSE Volume Ratio Secret Weapon, which is a leading indicator, volume is a confirming indicator when used normally.

I use the New York Stock Exchange (NYSE) volume in my analysis. If you're in the business of trading you know that the NYSE is a stock exchange located in New York City. Located at 11 Wall Street in Lower Manhattan, it is the world's largest stock exchange by market capitalization for the companies it represents. The average daily trading value is approximately $650 billion.

THE NYSE'S SECRET WEAPON: USING ITS VOLUME TO YOUR ADVANTAGE

I use the NYSE up and down volume to measure market sentiment, which is basically a way to gauge the fear and greed of the majority of market participants. By simply dividing the up volume by the down volume (or vice-versa), you create a ratio indicator that shows you when everyone is buying or selling shares. Think of it as people are being greedy or fearful. This is a powerful tool because it helps in identifying tradable short-term market tops and bottoms. This allows us to enter, re-enter or lock partial profits within a current trend.

These volume waves of greed and fear allow us to identify peaks and troughs during a sideways trading market. When used in conjunction with trend, cycle, and volatility analysis, this secret weapon dramatically improves your market timing while filtering out false tops and bottoms, which most traders fall victim to picking.

This is not something that many other traders follow. But in my opinion this indicator is critical in order to get a feel for the current sentiment (mindset/emotional level) of the market participants. Remember, we want to know what the herd is thinking. This way, when they are rushing in the door to buy or rushing the exit door to sell, we will be ready to take the other side of their emotionally driven trade.

NYSE SELLING STRENGTH IS YOUR BUYING OPPORTUNITY: DOWN VOLUME / UP VOLUME

This calculation tells us the ratio of sellers to buyers on any given day in real time. It is calculated by taking the NYSE down volume and dividing it by the up volume. It measures panic selling, and it acts as a contrarian indicator. Panic selling to me is when the majority of participants are overly bearish and fearful of the market. This causes large waves of selling, warning us that prices are likely moving too far in one direction. Price will likely give back some or all of the recent move that was created by this emotional surge of volume.

When this indicator is above 3, it means there are three times more shares being sold than there are being bought on the NYSE. This tells us that the majority of traders (the herd) are running for the exit door and selling their positions. The higher this indicator moves, or the longer it stays above 3, the more potential there is for a sharp rebound in price.

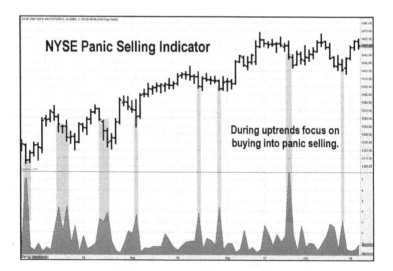

NYSE BUYING STRENGTH IS YOUR SELLING OPPORTUNITY: UP VOLUME / DOWN VOLUME

This calculation tells us the ratio of buyers to sellers on any given day in real-time.

It is calculated by taking the NYSE up volume and dividing it by the down volume. It measures panic buying and acts as a contrarian indicator. To me, greed-based buying is when the majority of participants are overly bullish on the market. This causes large waves of buying and short covering in the market, warning us that prices are likely moving up to fast. Thus, price will likely give back some or all of the recent gain that took place during the greed-induced volume surge.

When this indicator rises above 3 it means there are three times more buyers than sellers. This tells us that the majority of traders (the herd) are buying. Obviously the higher this indicator moves, or the longer it stays above 3, the more potential there is for a sharp reversal to the down side.

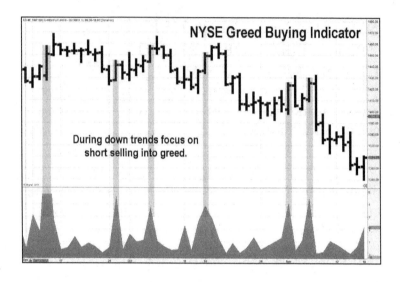

PYRAMID UP DURING FEAR & GREED

Earlier I mentioned the book "Market Wizards," which interviewed the world's top traders. One of the golden nuggets I took away from that book was not to average down, but to average up (pyramid). It's simple and makes sense, though most traders I know do not do this, and I never hear anyone else ever talking about it. Think about it, would you rather buy more shares of a stock that is falling in price and your trading account losses are compounding, or would you rather buy more of a stock which keeps rising in value and your trading account gains are increasing at a faster and faster rate? Of course we would rather put our money into an investment that will make us more money; that is common sense.

Trading is a tough game to win. We all lose trades, and at times we go through losing streaks that can be difficult.

The market is ruthless, so if a trade starts to go against you, getting stopped out of the trade could be the best thing for that trade. You need to add to winning positions and lock in partial profits along the way. If you do not lock in profits, the market will eventually take them back and then some.

CHAPTER 13

WHAT TO TRADE & THE CORRECT INSTRUMENT

What's stopping you from being even more successful as a trader?

Now is the time to analyze where you've been, see where you're going, and uncover any blind spots you might have. You need to do this in order to properly execute trades and select the correct trading instruments to reach your goals successfully.

When you have a few winning trades and things are going really well, or after a few losing trades when you start second guessing your trading strategy, have you ever found yourself taking risky trades outside of your regular trading routine? Or can you step back, regroup and tell yourself that this is just a part of trading? Can you keep your emotions in check and continue to follow your trading strategy because you know your system will eventually bring rewards?

Sometimes even the most successful traders become overconfident as a result of profitable trades, and their expectations rise to unhealthy levels. In the excitement of success and profits, they drift from their winning strategy. Without sound judgment and rules to safely navigate the financial market, they find themselves on the wrong side of the market with an oversized loss. This could have been avoided if they stuck to their plan.

Good examples of overconfidence from both novice and professional traders can be found in the bull market of 1995-2000, 2003-2008, and the most recent bull market. Traders and investors simply bought and held stocks during these times. With mounting profits and growing confidence, they continued to buy more shares and watched their accounts grow, forgetting that paper profits are not the same as realized profits.

This simple buy-and-hold strategy produced some amazing gains for those who were willing to try it. The gains generated from the bull market had most traders and investors mistakenly feeling invulnerable, and they thought that their strategy would continue to work for many years to come. Eventually each of the secular bull markets topped, and the financial market collapsed faster than most were ready to handle.

The recent purchases quickly turned into dramatic losses, and the market participants were in denial. They continued to hold and did not let go of hope. When the markets failed to recover, their losses became fixed as the bear market continued. Their financial bliss became a retirement nightmare.

Understanding the market life cycle and having the proper tools to identify which stage it is trading at provides you with powerful insight. It allows you to leverage the market with minimal risk through the use of various investment vehicles.

The important thing to remember is to analyze your emotions, your blind spots and your past patterns so you're not a trader who gets stuck in the trap of trading with emotions. Follow your trading strategy rules because it should put the odds in your favor for winning over the long run. Maintain a steady mind and trading routine.

"Set Trading Rules

Execute Trading Rules

Repeat"

HOW DO YOU KNOW WHAT INVESTMENT VEHICLE TO USE?

Most investors hold a diverse variety of investment vehicles in their portfolios. Investment vehicles can be low-risk, such as certificates of deposit (CDs) or bonds, or they can carry a greater degree of risk (such as with stocks, options and futures). Other types of investment vehicles include annuities, collectibles (art or coins, for example), mutual funds and exchange-traded funds (ETFs). Which one is right for you and your trading strategies?

TRADING INSTRUMENTS

In this chapter we will present some strategies and investment vehicles relevant to bullish, bearish and sideways trending markets.

As we begin our discussion about different trading instruments and strategies, we will use our INNER-Market Analysis trading signals to determine the direction to trade. It also will help us determine more precise entry, targets and exit points.

INDEX TRADING WITH EXCHANGE TRADED FUNDS (ETF'S)

These funds are easy to trade. They trade like stocks but are designed to mimic the price movement of a specific underlying investment. These funds were created to provide traders with the option to trade the movement of an index like the S&P 500 without having the thousands of dollars required to trade the futures market.

Here, for each share of the ETF purchased, you literally own a fractional share of the underlying equities of the index. These shares can be traded like a stock (at any time without additional restriction) and can even be traded in pre and post market extended hours.

Leveraged ETFs

There are now leveraged ETFs available, giving you 2x and 3x the percent move of the underlying index. For example, if the S&P 500 or SPY ETF moves up 1 percent and you had bought the 3x leveraged fund, your ETF would move up 3 percent.

Inverse ETF's

Many traders and investors do not like to short the market, and an even larger group doesn't even know what shorting means. Shorting the market means you are borrowing shares from your broker and sell them in the open market. You hope to buy them back at a lower price, return them to the broker and pocket the difference in value for a profit. If you don't understand this concept, do not worry. There is no need for shorting anymore because there are now inverse ETF's allowing you to profit from a falling stock market. These ETF's move up in value as the stock market falls. All you do is buy an inverse fund (which is also available with 1x, 2x, and 3x leverage) and watch the price move higher in your favor as the stock market falls.

Consider how ETF's could be played using our market analysis signals.

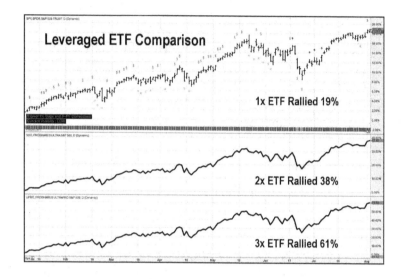

These ETF's follow the movement of the S&P 500 index, and as you can see, they move the same. The only difference is that the leveraged funds move in multiples of the underlying index.

As you can see from the previous chart, our INNER-Market signals present very timely, low-risk trading signals for the S&P 500 index. In that example, each trade followed the trend of the Swing Cycle. On average, this trend and its trades can last between four and twelve weeks.

For a shorter term trade, we would focus on the Momentum Cycle. Because market moves become smaller from a percentage point of view as we drop down to shorter cycles and timeframes, we typically use more leverage to generate a reasonable rate of return. To generate the returns we want, we can use a 2x or 3x leveraged ETF.

OPTIONS TRADING ON ETF'S & HIGH BETA STOCKS

When using options, it is important to exit trades quickly because they are highly leveraged and lose value over time.

We would normally use at-the-money options for optimal leverage, and we would generally select options with at least three or more months of remaining time. The purpose of this extra time is to limit the amount of time decay that can occur during the holding period.

In this instance, if we utilized the same trades using INNER-Market Analysis Signals, we simply need to modify our approach with another type of trading instrument (options) and exit more quickly. The results are dramatic. For example, if the SPY 1x leveraged ETF moved up 5 percent, we can boost our profit to 100 percent return in a much shorter period of time.

Index options are one of the simplest strategies to profit from the market's direction. No stock or ETF ownership is involved; it is purely an option play on markets, and it always settles to cash. The advantage of trading options is that the moves tend to be highly leveraged and swift. The disadvantage is that they tend to be a little pricier than tracking stock options. They also are more susceptible to time decay, as they can burn up a lot of time premium before a significant move may occur.

Options are a great way to profit from the market if you have a small account size. They allow you to profit in both up and down trending markets.

DYNAMIC MUTUAL FUNDS—RYDEX

Several mutual funds are available that offer the investor a remarkable ability to make money in up or down markets. Some of these can also provide leveraged returns, and some funds move inverse to the overall market direction. To generate profits in up markets, these funds use futures and options contracts. To generate profits in down markets, they will short sell securities and also employ futures and options contracts.

A favorite for many investors are the RYDEX dynamic funds. Investors seeking to include specific market exposures in their portfolios can access dozens of RYDEX Strategies. Each follows a specific index or sectors benchmark, and there are also leveraged and inverse funds.

The key benefit with these funds is that each is a no-load fund, and if you are subscribed with them directly, there are no trading commissions, either. The opportunity for significant growth is as simple as following the INNER-Market Analysis Swing Cycles direction. Using our technical INNER-Market Signals will help make your decisions for switching fairly easy. Let's look at some trades using the S&P RYDEX funds.

At the end of December, our analysis generated a buy signal on the 28th, and from that point, the stock market rallied. Let's review the chart and see how the RYDEX funds performed during that market rally.

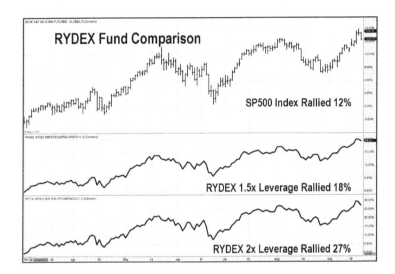

Notice how the RYDEX funds mirror the underlying investment (which is this case is the S&P 500 Index). The only difference between them is the amount of leverage you want to trade with. RYDEX funds have 1x, 1.5x and 2x leverage investments, which allows you to manage your portfolio's risk during times of different overall market volatility levels. The general rule is that the higher the market volatility (VIX), the less leverage you should use when trading. This will help offset the larger than normal price fluctuations that take place during times of uncertainty.

While the example shows prices trending higher, keep in mind you have the same options to buy inverse funds during a falling market or the same options to counter trends. These inverse funds rise as the stock market falls. So if the S&P 500 falls 5 percent you could be pocketing a 5 percent, 7.5 percent or 10 percent profit while most market participants are losing money. This is very exciting stuff, to say the least.

HIGH BETA STOCKS

As talked about earlier, three out of four stocks move with the broad market, just as a rising tide lifts all boats. But finding stocks that will move in concert with the markets requires some additional research.

Here we are looking for stocks which are helping to create the market's overall direction. In other words, the stocks we seek should mimic the movement of the market.

There are several ways this can be achieved, but a simple way is to look for stocks that have a high Beta. Beta is a measurement of a stock's performance relative to the overall market. A Beta of 1 means a stock's price and the broad market move about the same on a percentage basis.

For example, if the S&P 500 moves up one percent, a stock with a beta of 1 should have also moved up one percent.

A lower Beta suggests that the stock underperforms the market. For our purpose of trading, we will look for stocks that outperform the market. Look at high beta stocks as stocks with an attitude. Their price movements are exaggerated, and they will provide a somewhat leveraged opportunity for us.

For example: if a stock has a beta of 3, a five percent move in the market could produce a 15 percent gain in the stock. This is a great way of getting more bang for the buck without incurring the risk of using margin or worrying about the time decay that options have.

There are several financial websites and many charting and scanning platforms that allow you to search and sort stocks by their beta. Keep in mind that high beta stocks will change over time, so what was once a beta of 2 or 3 beta a year ago is likely not a high beta stock anymore. It could actually be a very low beta.

We'll use our INNER-Market analysis signals to help us know when to enter a trade, but we will use high beta stocks as our strategy to capture bigger profits. We'll start with the signal that formed in December again to keep things simple and comparative with other trading instruments.

Take a look at the S&P 500 (SPY) index fund verses the high beta stock (BAC). This chart shows that when we have our INNER-Market analysis buy signals, the high beta stock rockets higher in our favor.

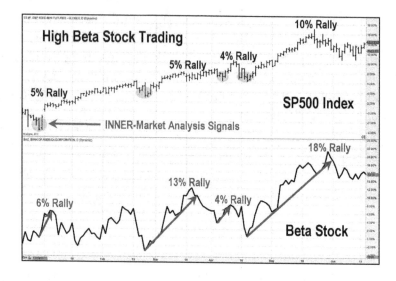

The chart above shows the percentage price swings that high beta stocks generate during oversold and overbought market conditions. While the S&P 500 on average moved up 4 percent to 5 percent within a few days, the high beta stock moved 4 percent, 13 percent and even continued to rally to 18 percent on the last signal.

In each case, you can see that by using higher beta stocks at critical bottoms, they can help you easily outperform the markets without adding much risk. Be aware, however, that you don't want to overstay your welcome. High beta stocks can move fast in both directions, so it is imperative that you manage positions based on the INNER-Analysis oversold and overbought signals.

ALTERNATIVE TRADING INSTRUMENTS

Depending on your trading experience and your country's regulations, you may be trading some of these other highly leveraged instruments like Futures, Spread Betting or CFD's. Each of these instruments vary in terms of market requirements and available leverage. But each has an instrument that will mimic some of the high beta stocks of the major stock market averages, like the S&P 500, DOW, NASDAQ and Russell 2K. If you do not know what these instruments are, I've provided you with a short description of each.

FUTURES EXPLAINED

This is a standard contract between two parties to buy or sell an asset in the future for a price agreed upon today. Futures contracts are typically based around indexes or commodities. Depending on the contract you are trading, it may settle in cash, or there could be physical delivery of the goods. Futures trading is for advance traders and investors only, and it must be thoroughly understood before attempting to trade.

SPREAD BETTING EXPLAINED

Spread Betting is a type of speculation that involves taking a bet on the price movement of a security. A spread betting company quotes two prices, the bid and offer price (also called the spread), and investors then bet whether the price of the underlying security will be lower than the bid or higher than the offer. The investor does not own the underlying stock in spread betting, they simply speculate on the price movement of the stock, commodity or index.

CONTRACT FOR DIFFERENCE (CFD)

CFD is the abbreviated term for a contract for difference. A CFD is a contract between two parties to exchange the difference between the entry and exit price of a financial instrument. CFD traders can invest on domestic and global shares as well as foreign exchange indices and commodities.

Because CFD's are derivatives, you never own the physical share or commodity; instead you either profit or lose on the underlying share price movement, as the CFD mirrors the price of the underlying security. As a result of never actually owning the security, you are not entitled to any voting rights.

As well as buying a CFD (going long) with the view that it may rise, you can also sell a CFD (short sell) with the view that it may fall.

Money and risk management are two skills you will need to master. You will also need to carefully manage your interest costs, trades and margin calls to ensure these do not rise to a level which would force you to close positions.

To reduce your risk, it is strongly recommended that you use stop-losses when trading CFD's. These are orders, set at a pre-determined price at the beginning of the trade, which will trigger an exit order when the CFD passes through this set price. It limits the extent of your loss to some degree.

No matter what investment vehicle you decide to focus on, learning the relationship between the market and the vehicle—and understanding the strategy you'll deploy—is key. Eliminate blind spots by being aware of where you've been and any errors you've made thus far. Keep refining your system. The INNER-Market Analysis will become an invaluable tool to your long-term success. You will know when those key turning points are developing in the markets, and better yet, how to anticipate them as you plan your next trades.

CHAPTER 14

TRADE MANAGEMENT STRATEGIES

E arlier in the book we talked about the danger of doing
nothing. Becoming an excellent trader requires a
fine balance of knowing when to move and when not to.
Analysis paralysis can lead to inactivity that sabotages your
momentum and profits. But there are times when sitting
on your hands and waiting is actually a good decision.

> "Men who can sit tight are uncommon. I found
> that it is one of the hardest things to learn, but it is
> only after a stock operator has firmly grasped this
> that he can make big money."

—Edwin Lefevre, *Reminiscences of a Stock Operator*

What does this mean?

1. Know when not to trade. Know when the market
   is untradeable, and wait for a setup. In trading you

will often hear the maxims "Trade with the trend" or the "Trend is your friend." Having a finely tuned trading strategy will help you with this.

2. Sit on a trade when it's going in your favor. Do not get me wrong here; I am a HUGE believer of taking partial profits when price moves in my favor. But you must continue to hold a core position because the trends are where you will make most of your money. They can last for extended periods of time.

MASTERING THE RUNNER

To make serious money trading while controlling your overall risk, you must first master "the runner." The runner is a portion of a position that you keep open for as long as possible when a trade is moving in your favor. As the trading maxim says, "Cut your losses, and let your profits run." It sounds simple enough, but executing the runner principle is challenging. To understand why, we'll look at how the most minimalist trade, buying only one contract, can be suboptimal.

Let's say a one lot (one contract, one share) trade goes in a trader's direction, and let's say the trader exits for a profit. If the market continues to move in the original direction, the trader regrets closing his position. Sometimes this emotional regret leads to a bad decision to re-enter, and in most cases it's too late. Price has already made a substantial move, and the overall risk of a reversal or sharp pullback has increased dramatically. A disciplined trader who follows a specific strategy, however, will use multiple lots but scale out.

Let's say you enter a position that can be broken up into two portions. As the market moves in your favor and your analysis is telling you to take some profits, you can exit the first half of your position for a profit. This immediately eliminates your emotional need to lock in gains. If you were to move your protective stop to the break-even point, you would now have a trade that is profitable. This allows you to let the market continue to run in your direction until the trend is over.

The challenge is holding onto that runner. And you should, because one risk-free runner can be worth a lot more than several of your next full-risk trades combined.

There are several ways to determine when to lock in partial profits and exit your runners. You can use technical analysis (the use of support, resistance, trend lines, previous peaks or troughs, moving averages, etc.) OR a simple trailing stop OR INNER-Market analysis signals coupled with a trailing stop. These allow you to squeeze out the most profit per trade before price reverses direction.

YOUR EXIT STRATEGY

For most traders, entering a position is no problem. The exit, however, is by far more difficult. I use four different types of exit strategies for my trading, and these are basic common stops available with all brokers across the board.

Every trader should be using at least one type of stop, if not a combination of several of them.

As I will briefly discuss below, there are different types of stops to use when managing positions. I would first like to mention that through INNER-Market analysis, our stop placement is not based on where the general public (who is using single-price analysis) would be placing their stops. They typically place their stops at levels exceeding support, resistance levels or breaks of trend lines, etc. Because we have more insight on where price has been and should be headed in the near future, we are able to place our stops just out of range from where the market will try to run the stops before reversing back in our favor.

The initial stop is your insurance against big losses and is by far the most important aspect in trading. You shouldn't enter a trade without knowing exactly where your initial stop is. Not placing a hard stop, meaning entering your stop order so it is out there in the market, is the biggest reason for loss of trading capital and for the potential failure in your trading business.

People who take partial gains sell their position after the first reasonable move in their favor. A reasonable move would be a move into a resistance area (for longs). This resistance can be of technical or psychological nature. Partial gains play an important role in my trading. I've seen many of the most successful traders taking partial gains because the results are powerful.

Partial Profits and Break-Even Stops: break even means to set the stop at the price where you initially entered the position. I start using break-even stops once the position has successfully risen a significant amount. If a short term cycle is topping, I lock in partial profits by selling a portion of my trade while holding onto a portion as a runner. I hold onto the runner in case the trend continues for several more days, weeks or months.

Trailing Stops: these are a great way to manage runners. Trailing stops can be traded in many different ways. Some traders manually adjust their stops under the most recent pivot lows, and others use a set dollar amount which allows the stop to follow the price. You also can use a percent trading stop, which means your stop will follow the price higher. For example, you could set a stop that is 3 percent below the highest price.

When I am trading the S&P 500, once I have taken my partial gains (which is typically around the one to two percent gain area), I move my protective stop to a break-even point. When my trade moves in my favor by 3 percent, I switch to a 3 percent trailing stop. As price moves up, so does my stop. This allows us to ride the trend for larger gains, and it allows us not have to manage the last portion of the position. The trailing stop is going to close the position when the trend reverses and triggers the stop.

TRADE MANAGEMENT

Know what you're going to do before you do it. That's called having a strategy.

The INNER-Market Analysis tool I created makes it easy. It can do all these things for the user, including entry price, partial profit, initial stop and trailing stop. When a trend has reversed, it can close out the balance of any long positions.

Entering trades is simple; watching the market for new trade setups or watching your runner without exiting the trade early is hard. While trading is not that difficult when you have a proven trading system, know that managing open positions is part art and part science. It will take some time to master. But once you know what you're going to do before you do it, you've got a huge advantage over the majority of market participants.

CHAPTER 15

THE PARADIGM SHIFT FROM FINANCIAL ADVISORS TO ALGORITHMIC TRADING SYSTEMS

O ver the last 50 plus years, people have been using the same methods of investing for their future, and not much has really changed. The norm of hiring a financial advisor to plop your money into generic mutual funds, RYDEX funds and insurance plans (while taking a 2 percent annual fee on your life savings) has been good enough for the masses. Because it's the norm and what everyone has and is doing, we naturally think that it's the right thing to do with our money. But is good enough really GOOD ENOUGH for you?

Think about it. You work hard, save money, plan for your future and hire a financial advisor to guide you through the shark-infested waters of investing so you can live your dream. But what really happens? You hand over your money, and you put your trust and future into the hands of someone who simply follows an old-school way of investing. This method is loaded with front-end fees, back-end fees and annual fees. And in most cases, it does not make you money during market downturns!

Your retirement money isn't protected in the event of a market crash or multi-year bear market. So what happens? You end up riding the financial roller coaster, which is something you don't really want to do (or do again for that matter). But you do it because it's the only way you know and the way everyone else has done it.

The industry average is roughly one percent, but fees can range from 0.80 percent to two percent in the U.S. and Canada. Typically the more assets you have, the lower the fee. While that may not sound like much up front, don't forget that most of these funds they put your money into also have roughly another one percent annual fee. This extra percent you pay makes a big difference in your long-term return.

For example, an investor with a $250,000 portfolio earning seven percent per year would be sitting on $967,000 after 20 years. Had they paid an advisor using mutual funds with a two percent percent fee of their assets during those years, however, their account value would fall to $663,000—a difference of roughly $304,000.

So, the financial advisor who likely didn't protect or make you money (although he or she might be a perfectly nice, competent professional with excellent intentions) during the multiple bear markets that you would have encountered made away with a good chunk of your nest egg. They did this with virtually no downside risk to them;

they get paid every year no matter what the financial market does, whether they made you any money or not.

Does that sound like a plan you want to stick with going forward?

It doesn't to me.

The two most important things you can do to improve the performance of your portfolio is to reduce your trading fees and to have a proven strategy that makes money in a bear market.

This old-school way of investing for your future—without downside protection and without a trading strategy for your money during market crashes and bear markets—is just that. Old school.

Today, you can do things differently. You can use proven algorithmic trading/investing strategies. This not only allows you to potentially avoid market crashes and multi-year bear markets, but you can actually profit from them handsomely. Algorithm trading systems are starting to gain traction with the average investor because the old way of doing things doesn't make sense.

People are finally starting to communicate more about their financial situation and experiences, and they are realizing they've had the exact same financial outcome and ridden the same emotional roller coaster. This realization has triggered individuals to gain a better understanding of what happened, and more are starting to see the new ways money can and should be managed. In short, they are having an epiphany. Epiphanies are relatively rare occurrences, and they generally follow a process of significant thought about a problem. They are often triggered by new information, processes and tools that are available.

So what does all this mean?

The investment world is about to have a paradigm shift. It means the old-school way of investing is being challenged with newer, more sophisticated, proven, rule-based strategies that perform well in all market conditions. These systems also automatically manage positions and risk for your maximum benefit and income potential.

In order to truly understand Boom-Bust Cycles (paradigm shifts), you'll need to review the work of Carlota Perez (especially her book Technological Revolutions and Financial Capital). In this work, you can see how economic paradigms rise and fall.

Perez explains an interesting phenomenon: that every 50 years or so, there have been new economic structures that caused the collapse of what came before. Perez identified five economic paradigms (or "Great Surges") throughout this period:

- Industrial Revolution in Britain (1770-1830)

- Age of Steam and Railways (1830-1870)

- Age of Steel, Electricity and Heavy Engineering (1870-1920)

- Age of Oil, Automobiles and Mass Production (1920-1975)

- Age of Information and Telecommunications (1975-20??)

- The use of Financial Advisors and Mutual Funds (1970-20??)

Each of these times represents a major technological breakthrough. These breakthroughs resulted in a fundamental restructuring of how things were done. Each of these periods had its own paradigms for wealth-generation, institutional structures, regulatory environments and desired trajectories for society. The technologies themselves were only one piece of the vital inputs that ultimately defined each era.

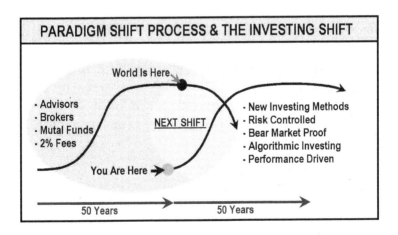

BE AWARE OF PARADIGM PARALYSIS

Perhaps the greatest barrier to a paradigm shift is the reality of paradigm paralysis. This is the inability or refusal to see beyond the current models of thinking, and it is similar to what psychologists call confirmation bias. A couple examples would be the rejection of Galileo's theory of a heliocentric universe and the discovery of electrostatic photography. Across history, there have been many errors in thinking and many traditional processes that were maintained by the crowd simply because there wasn't yet a better way. Then along came a Henry Ford or some other innovative individual and one was created. There is a better way to investing, and now is the time to get on the path.

THE SHIFT IS HAPPENING NOW

In the year 2010, more than 70 percent of the stock shares traded on the NYSE and NASDAQ were generated from automated trading systems. Today it's much higher, and it is continuing to grow. Most of these systems are done by large institutions, but individuals with their own trading system are a category growing at an incredible rate each year.

Traders and investors can now turn precise entry, exit and money management rules into automated trading systems. This allows computers to execute, monitor and manage positions.

The biggest attraction of automated strategies is that it eliminates some of the emotion from trading. Since trades are automatically executed once a specific criterion has been met, emotion is taken out of the equation This next section will educate and explain some of the advantages and disadvantages, as well as the realities, of automated trading systems.

WHAT IS AN AUTOMATED TRADING SYSTEM?

Automated trading systems, also referred to as mechanical trading systems, algorithmic trading, automated trading, block-box trading, or system trading, allow traders to create specific sets of rules for both trade entries and exits that, once programmed, can be automatically executed via a computer. Each trade rule can be based on simple conditions, such as a moving average crossover, or each trade can be more complicated by using an individual's proprietary indicator, ratios and data points. Automated trading systems typically require the use of trading software capable of running the trading systems' code and trade execution.

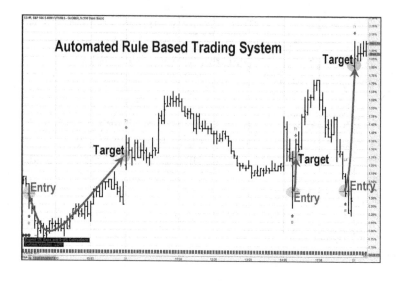

Above: A 5-minute chart of the ES contract with an automated strategy applied.

Once the system rules have been established, the trading platform can monitor the market or a specific investment you intend to trade for entry and exit points based on the trading strategy specifications. In general when a trade is executed, orders for protective stop losses and profit targets will automatically be created and executed. During volatile fast moving markets, automated order entry can mean the difference between a profit and a loss.

ADVANTAGES OF AUTOMATED TRADING SYSTEMS

Ability to Backtest. Backtesting allows us to apply trading rules to historical market data. This tests allows us to determine the viability of an idea. When building a system for automated trading, all rules need to be absolute, with no room for interpretation. Computers cannot make guesses and must be told exactly what to do for each and every possible scenario. Careful backtesting allows us to evaluate and fine-tune a trading idea. Backtesting also determines the system's expectancy going forward. Important data points you should track are your average maximum dollar drawdown, your average winning trade amount, your average losing trade amount and your percentage of trades that are winners.

Achieve Consistency. One of the biggest challenges in trading is to plan the trade and to trade the plan. Even if a trading plan has the potential to be profitable, traders who ignore the rules are altering any expectancy the system would have had. Losing trades can be psychologically traumatizing, so a trader who has two or three losing trades in a row might decide to skip the next trade. Automated trading systems allow traders to achieve consistency by trading the plan.

Improved Order Entry Speed. Since computers can respond instantly, automated systems are able to trigger orders as soon as a set of trade rules are met. Getting in or out of a trade a few seconds earlier can make a big difference in the trade's outcome. This is especially true over a long period of time when hundreds or even thousands of trades have been taken.

Minimize Emotions. Automated trading systems minimize emotions throughout the trading process. By keeping their emotions in check, traders typically have an easier time sticking to the plan. Because trades are executed automatically, you will not be able to hesitate or question the trade. Those who are either afraid to pull the trigger and those who are more apt to overtrade benefit greatly from an automated system.

Preserve Discipline. With trading rules already established and trade execution performed automatically, discipline is preserved even during volatile market conditions. Discipline in most cases is lost due to the fear and greed factor. The fear of taking a loss, or the desire to squeeze out a little more profit from a trade, hurts discipline. In addition, pilot error is minimized, and an order to buy 500 shares will not be incorrectly entered as an order to buy 5000 shares, for example.

Diversify Trading. Automated trading systems allow us to trade multiple accounts and various strategies at the same time. This has the potential to spread risk over various instruments and timeframes. What would be incredibly difficult for a trader to accomplish can be efficiently executed by a computer in a matter of milliseconds.

DISADVANTAGES AND REALITIES OF AUTOMATED TRADING SYSTEMS

Automated trading systems boast many advantages, but there are some downfalls and realties of which you should be aware.

Mechanical Failures. While automated trading in theory seems simple: set up the trading software, program the rules and watch it trade. The reality, however, is automated trading is a sophisticated method of trading but not infallible. Depending on how the system creator has the entire process set up, a trade order could reside on an individual computer and not a server. If this is the case, an order might not be sent to the market when an Internet connection is lost. There could also be a discrepancy between the "theoretical trades" generated by the strategy and the order-entry platform component that turns them into real trades. Individuals new to the automated trading arena should expect a learning curve when building, testing and running their first few systems. It is generally a good idea to start with small trade sizes while the process is refined.

System Monitoring. Although it would be great to turn on the computer in the morning and walk away for the day, automated trading systems require monitoring. Because of the potential for mechanical failures, such as internet-connectivity issues, power losses, computer crashes or system idiosyncrasies, it is possible for an automated trading system to experience anomalies. These could result in errant orders, missing orders or duplicate orders. If the system is monitored, these events can be identified and resolved quickly.

Over-Optimization. Though not specific to automated trading systems, traders who employ backtesting techniques can create systems that look great on paper and perform terribly with a live market. Over-optimization refers to excessive curve-fitting that produces a trading strategy that is unreliable. It is easy to create and tweak a strategy that achieves exceptional results on historical data. You must be aware of all the known issues with backtesting to be sure your new plan has been built to work within the backtesting guidelines for accuracy. If you do not, you may end up with over-optimization systems that look good on paper only.

SERVER-BASED AUTOMATED SYSTEMS

Traders do have the option to run their automated trading systems with a server-based host. Operating your trading platform and system on a dedicated server provides you with a potentially faster and more reliable platform. This minimizes unnecessary platform crashes and server failure or loss of internet, and it improves your order execution times.

Being able to leave your trading software running 24/7, not worrying about restarting applications, reloading strategies or filling in missing tick data, is a huge benefit if you plan to operate your own automated trading system.

HOW TO TAKE ADVANTAGE OF THE TRADING AND INVESTING SHIFT

The power lies in the masses ... and you and millions of others who have been using the old-school method of trading and investing (and are just now reaching the breaking point) should say enough is enough!

With so much information available, it is just a matter of time before average investors start demanding performance from their advisors. Most advisors are not technical analysts and cannot read into the charts, nor can they provide you with automated trading systems that are both backtested and forward tested. Most do not have multiple trading strategies within to profitably trade bull, bear and sideways trading markets.

Automated trading is about to explode, and when it does, the doors will open for investors around the world to allocate portions of their trading accounts or investment capital to specific systems and strategies traded for them in their brokerage account. Get ready to do things a better way.

CHAPTER 16

WHERE DO YOU GO FROM HERE?

Now that you've read through this book, you're probably feeling a lot wiser, stronger and more confident (as well as a bit anxious and excited), ready to go out and build a trading strategy that works for you! Maybe you've already put this book down once or twice to apply some of the indicators we talked about. Congratulations on making a commitment to a rewarding journey.

As with all things in life, having clarity with a plan and your goal gives you purpose and the drive to keep learning and improving your skills. Creating rule-based trading strategies for various market conditions and executing each trade without letting your emotions get in the way should be your focus and goal.

It took me years to figure out, learn and master what I have shared with you in this book. I almost gave up on trading many times when I was first starting out. But my passion for trading the financial markets and for achieving the lifestyle it could provide me always empowered me to get back up and try again. Each time I hit one of these walls of frustration, I learned something new about who I am and how my brain functions – along with my trading weaknesses. Once I knew my weaknesses, I focused on creating trading strategies which worked within my comfort zones and kept my emotions under control to overcome them. A detailed, step-by-step trading strategy changed the way I traded in a way I never thought possible. Trades are now a simple "YES, enter trade now," or "NO, I should stay in cash." Remember, "Passion NEVER Fails."

The information in this book was designed to empower you to go out on your own and become an independent trader, or, if you already were one of these, to become as wildly successful as you can be! Some of the things you've learned include:

- Knowing Yourself and what strategy is for you

- The four market stages and how to trade them

- The paradox of emotions, such as greed and fear

- Market psychology and the mentality of the herd

- Overcoming mental blockers, like analysis paralysis

- How to Identify Trends

- How to use cycles to forecast price and trade duration

- Volume/Price relationship

- Investment vehicles

- Mastering the Runner

- The importance of position management and an exit strategy

- Observe price-action and don't let emotions drive your trading

- Don't trade out of anger or frustration. The market will punish you for out of control emotional trades.

- Relax and have fun. You don't always need to be in a position, and cash is king.

Learning all you can about market psychology and the way markets work will help you gain the advantage you need to confidently trade.

Utilize tools and the power of our INNER-Market Analysis system and save yourself time, money, errors and frustration. Through our tools and programs, you can benefit from our market research and forecasting accuracy. Although nothing's 100 percent, these tools give you a distinct advantage. You won't have to start from square one. You'll be armed with the information and confidence you need to perfect your market timing, your forecasting and your trading skills.

As a trader, think of yourself as a risk manager. Continually reassess risk, and continually adjust your profit targets and protective stops. Always know what you're going to do before you do. This will keep emotion from creeping in, which will steal or limit profits, break your trading rules and undermine all your hard work.

Follow the rules and tips you've learned, use our analysis tools, take our trading strategy course and join The Technical Traders free newsletter. This will help you stay up to speed on current market trends, opportunities and educational information.

Once you're finished taking our programs "Trading As Your Business", "Trading System Mastery," and our simple visual drag and drop "Automated Trading Strategy Builder" building your own customized trading strategies will be simple. You will be armed with a detailed, step-by-step trading system, and you will have the confidence and drive to trade while living the lifestyle you always wanted. More information is listed at the back of this book.

But why learn to build a race car when all you want to do is drive it? Well, now you can. All of our technical trading tools are available, so you can have our complete proven system running live on your computer. Through our training videos, trading system and its trading signals, all that is left to do is the execution of the trades.

Learn More: www.thetechnicaltraders.com/tools/

On the other hand, if you are not the type or simply do not want to spend the time to place trades, then use our Automated INNER-Market Analysis Trading System—AlgoTrades. Everything we talked about in this book—the best proven trading strategies, market timing, optimal trade entry/exits and position management—is at your fingertips. And best of all, the trades are done for you automatically in your brokerage account. You don't have to lift a finger or worry about what the market is doing ever again.

Learn More: www.AlgoTrades.net

TRADING SYSTEM MASTERY SUMMARY

Ever since I began trading, I've become more and more passionate about helping other traders learn and grow their skills. My excitement for trading continues to grow each year, and I suspect it'll be the same way for you. Once you gain momentum, it's addicting and rewarding like no other business. It's like owning your own business with a machine to print money, and all you have to do is keep your eye on the machine for when trade setups are generated. Then you hit the print button (enter a trade) and get to see how much money it will put into your trading account.

As talked about in a previous chapter, you can have several trading strategies. Each one pulls money out of the market differently depending on if it is based on a different time frame (like the weekly, daily or intraday chart or one that you use during different market conditions). I see each of these strategies as being a printing press for making money. This is why our Automated-INNER-Market Trading System—AlgoTrades—has multiple trading strategies that power it, and this is how it generates results in all market conditions.

I've worked hard to research the market, and I have lived and breathed trading to give you the most current understanding of the financial market as a whole. My trading research is clear and simple, not complex. Complexity is never good because it leads to confusion, and there's no place for that in your trading strategy.

My analysis process and tools allow you to spot where the market is trading in terms of the four market stages and its current trend. The process and tools also allow you to spot where it is most likely to move next and when to enter and manage trades. INNER-Market Analysis will dramatically eliminate trading on emotions, and it will make investing clear, exciting and profitable.

Appendices

INNER-MARKET ANALYSIS
FORECASTING TOOLS & BENEFITS

RULES, TIPS & TRICKS

KEY TECHNICAL TRADING RULES

TOP 16 TRADING TIPS

TRADING RESOURCES

INNER-MARKET ANALYSIS FORECASTING TOOLS & BENEFITS

How can utilizing trading tools and a developed system increase your chances for success? The proper tools help you by providing valuable information as to where different parts (volume, sentiment, cycles, trends and volatility) are trading with a stock, sector, commodity or index.

In short, properly calibrated trading tools quickly and automatically put the odds in your favor, telling you if prices should be rising or falling in the coming days. They save you a lot of time by analyzing the various aspects of the market. They also provide you with peace of mind that the information has been calculated correctly.

INNER-Market Trend Tool—Identifies Stock Market Index Trends the moment a trade changes (Up, Sideways and Down).

Benefit: Knowing the direction of the market trend greatly improves your trading odds for success. This keeps your positions in favor of the overall market direction, and your position therefore will naturally want to move in your favor. Using a combination of data points based off of moving averages, cycles, volume and price patterns, our INNER-Market Trend Indicator saves you valuable time while keeping you and your money on the right side of the market.

INNER-Market Swing Trading Signals—Identifies key entry signals, partial profit taking signals and exit signals.

Benefit: These are deal trading signals for both investors and swing traders. No matter the market trend, this tool incorporates all aspects of the market to put the odds in your favor.

INNER-Market Intelligent Protective Stops

Benefit: Intelligent stops help avoid having your stop run by the market. Using a combination of data points and money management rules, the intelligent stops are automatically adjusted for maximum profits while limiting downside risk.

INNER-Market Momentum Trading Signals—Identifies intraday turning points in real-time.

Benefit: This is the ultimate day trader and momentum trader tool. Instead of using basic technical analysis for support and resistance levels (which is what that majority of traders use), this tool bases its analysis on the momentum cycle, volatility, volume flow, market sentiment and candlestick patterns.

So while the majority of traders are getting shaken out of the market as the market makers run the stops (piercing a recent low or high), our system is analyzing what the big money is doing. It waits for several data points to align before exiting a trade, entering a new position or locking in profits.

In short, the majority of traders use basic, single-price analysis for placing stops or locking in gains. We do not; we focus on real-time data, which tells us when the market is truly starting to shows signs of support or resistance. In many cases the market runs into sellers BEFORE price reaches the obvious resistance level. The good news is that we can see this and get out before price drops. Our analysis can also keep us in trades longer because when then there looks to be a resistance level on the chart, there may not be one at all. When this happens, we are able to ride positions for much larger gains while other traders are kicking themselves for getting out too early.

Our Tools Run On Award-Winning Charting Platforms

Benefit: No need to install and learn another charting platform. Instead, our analysis tools can be added to your favorite platform so you can begin using it right away.

This simple and easy-to-use trading tool does all of the analysis you need in seconds, and it runs as an end-of-day (EOD) swing trading system, real-time swing trading system and real-time day/momentum system.

Individuals who have full-time jobs can trade using the EOD (End-Of-Day) swing trading signals, allowing them and take advantage of the financial markets while they are at work. The EOD version is web-based, so you can access the information anytime from anywhere and place your trades for the open the next trading day.

Full-time traders can use both the real-time Swing and Momentum Trading system to improve their overall market timing on all their trading positions. Either way, this is a Must-Have Trading Tool if you want a steady stream of income while building wealth.

AlgoTrades—Automated Investing System

Benefit: Have our INNER-Market Analysis trading strategies automatically traded in your brokerage account without having to learn the financial market or follow it. Trades are executed in real-time without your involvement. It is a true, 100 percent algorithmic decision-making and order execution system. This solution can completely alleviate the hassles of staring at the computer monitor and being glued to the computer.

Learn More Here: www.AlgoTrades.net

RULES, TIPS & TRICKS

I've put together some key points which I think should be read a few times in order for these critical trading ideas to be stored in your subconscious for quick retrieval. It's like being a star quarterback in the NFL in the locker room rehearsing plays. You've learned the plays all week and studied them, and now it's time to execute. When you focus on executing a strategy, it is easier to keep your actions, trades and emotions in check.

Pulling money from the market on a daily, weekly or monthly basis is no easy task. Ninety-five percent of traders break-even or lose money year after year. Being able to follow the market without any directional bias is difficult, especially with so many online publications posting their analysis and opinions as to why the market should go up or down. While it is possible to predict and trade short-term movements, anything beyond a couple weeks will not be very accurate.

Traders and investors in general tend to react to news, events and chart patterns in a very predictable way. Once you understand what the average trader (the herd) is seeing and feeling on an emotional level, you can position yourself with high probability setups to take advantage of their bad habits. My INNER-Market Analysis strategies use a combination of indicators, cycle analysis, price action, volume and intraday market sentiment for doing just that.

I am a strong believer that cash is a great position to be in. I find that 77 percent of the time my active trading account is in cash, just waiting for short-term, high probability setups to unfold.

Hopefully this section has got you thinking about your trading strategy and emotional behaviors. Remember the market is always evolving, so learning to change with the times is crucial for long-term success.

Set aside any directional bias and opinions on the market you may have, and start creating your own strategies. Or if you cannot create your own, use a system that is already proven and start trading like an automated robot. If you do this, you will be following the trading rules that put the odds in your favor. Learn, grow and set realistic expectations; as with any new business, the learning curve produces peaks and valleys, and you may make mistakes along the way. Continue to learn and refine your process, as eventually it will be easy. Price rules. Trade what you see, and not what you or anyone else thinks. Analyze a variety of scenarios, and be prepared for anything!

KEY TECHNICAL TRADING RULES

B efore entering any trade, it is important to have an understanding of what the overall market conditions are like. Depending on market conditions, you will be focusing on more of a trending type of strategy or a shorter-term, momentum type trading strategy. The key is to wait for low risk/high probability setups to present themselves. If you wait for this, the odds are in your favor before taking a trade. Below are some key factors you should be aware of prior to taking a trade.

Finding a Low Risk/High Probability Setup:

- Trade in the direction of the longer term trend. I use the 20- or 50-day moving average on the daily chart.

- If the trend looks to be overextended and has not had a pullback in a while, trade with a smaller position size.

- If the market is at or near overhead resistance, trade with a smaller position size.

- Time your entries and exits using short-term timeframes like the 10- or 30-minute charts.

- Clearly identify an exit point for each trade prior to entering. Use support/resistance levels, pivot highs/lows and trend lines.

- Identify the first area where the trade will lose momentum (support/resistance) and look to take partial profits at that level. Then move your protective stop up accordingly.

- Take partial profits on the first sizable surge in your favor. This reduces emotions and downside risk, and it increases the number of winning trades you will make.

- Follow the price and volume. I always watch the volume using shorter term time frames like the one- and 10-minute charts. This gives me a feel if the larger orders are buys or sells. You can use the time and sales window with a filter that shows only futures orders of 20 contracts or more, and for stocks I filter out orders under 500 or 1000 shares (depending on the volume of the stock).

- You must have patience with winning trades because winners can run for days or even months. When in doubt, slowly scale out of position while locking in more gains as it continues to move in your favor.

- Create a detailed trading strategy, complete with trade setup criteria, trade management and execution rules. Then focus on following the system and refining it over time.

TOP 16 TRADING TIPS

#1. Only Price pays!

Know that the only thing that matters when trading is price.

#2. Volatility and Volume Are Your Warning Signal

Just before the market changes direction, we tend to see volatility and volume rise.

#3. Don't Wait For Volume

As important as volume is, do not wait for it confirm your decision. Buys and sells should be determined based on price action.

#4. Never Use Leveraged ETF's For Chart/ Trend Analysis

When analyzing the market, always use the underlying investment chart to locate trends and support/resistance levels. Leveraged ETF's lose value over time and also carry more intraday volatility. This results in false breakouts, support and resistance levels.

#5. We Are All Susceptible to Fear And Greed

Leveraging your position can also leverage these emotions to uncontrollable levels.

#6. Cash Is A Position

Some of the top traders only expose themselves to the market when there is a high probability of winning. If there is not, they remain safely in cash.

#7. Discipline and patience are your best traits; emotions are your enemy.

#8. Rely upon yourself

There are lots of great trading research newsletters and other advisory services. Find one or two that match your approach, and apply what you know to improve on it.

#9. Enter On The First Pause

The first pullback after a trend reversal or breakout is typically the best place and time to initiate a position.

#10. Finding It Hard To Get Long or Short The Market?

A general rule is if it's hard emotionally to buy into an uptrend, the market is going higher. If it's tough to sell short, it is likely going lower.

#11. Heavy Volume Sells

It is important to know that light volume trading sessions typically trade flat or trend higher overall. Selloffs in the market require strong, above average volume because there is a natural upward/buying bias in the market.

#12. Best Intraday Times To Trade

Focus on trading between 9:35 a.m. and 11:30 a.m. ET. That is when there are solid trends, heavy volume and the least amount of market manipulation. Step away at lunch, and start watching the market again between 2 p.m. and 4 p.m. ET when volume starts to pick back up.

#13. Protective Stops

It is important to always use protective stops. Have one placed in case of a market crash or in case you cannot access your broker. If you don't, eventually you will learn why you need them the hard way.

#14. Trade Defensive

The market has no mercy and will take every penny from you if you don't know what you are doing. While keeping a runner, move protective stops up and take partial profits on price surges in your favor.

#15. During heightened times of market uncertainty, retreat to short timeframes for trading and use less capital.

#16. Every Stock, Index, Commodity and Currency has a Unique Personality

If you think one strategy/software program can generate trading signals for the 7,000+ stocks and also generate signals for currencies, commodities, bonds and indexes, you are in for a rough ride. Also remember that each of the different chart time frames (like the 1 minute, 10 minute, 60 minute, daily, weekly etc.) will require its own trading strategy. So focus, specialize and master one security and one timeframe at a time!

TRADING RESOURCES

AlgoTrades
Automated algo-rithmic investing system.
www.AlgoTrades.net

The Technical Traders Tools
Proven indicators to identify trends, cycles, volatility, volume and market sentiment.
www.TheTechnicalTraders.com/tools/

Trading As Your Business
Brian McAboy's proven system to build a successful trading plan. Program:
www.TheTechnicalTraders.com/tradingasyourbusiness/

Trading System Mastery
Brian McAboy's step-by-step blueprint to creating winning trading strategies and backtesting.Program:
www.thetechnicaltraders.com/tradingsystemmastery/

Algorithmic Trading Strategy Builder
Build your trading strategies without a single line of code. Backtest, simulate, and trade directly through your broker. Software:
www.thetechnicaltraders.com/automatedstrategybuilder/

The Technical Traders
Trading articles, market commentary, daily trade ideas, free real-time charting, economic data, trading tools and much more.
www.TheTechnicalTraders.com

Chris Vermeulen's Free Stock Charts List
Chris shares his market insight and forecasts free online.
www.StockCharts.com/public/1992897

ABOUT THE AUTHOR

Chris Vermeulen is an experienced and successful trader, educator and author. Involved in the markets since 1997, he is the author of several financial trading and educational newsletters. He is also the founder of Technical Traders Ltd.

As an active trader and investor, Mr. Vermeulen soon recognized the huge potential that online investing and algorithmic trading systems held for individual investors. The development of Chris' Technical Trading Mastery resulted from his obsession with the market. Through years of research and testing, he created the AlgoTrades Investing system, which is quickly gaining popularity around the world.

Chris has been described as a "gifted technical analyst" who can navigate the financial markets in any market condition. His list of personal and professional relationships approaches 25,000, people with whom he connects and nourishes out of his passion for trading.

Chris has been interviewed, published or written about in *Futures Magazine, The Street, Trader Interview, Kitco, Financial Sense, Dick Davis Investment Digest* and hundreds of online sites.

THANK YOU GIFT VALUED AT $97

Get AlgoTrades Monthly Investor Reports FREE.

Stay ahead of the stock market...

Invest your way to financial freedom...

Everything you learned in this book has been applied to the financial market and summarized for your convenience in the Monthly Investor Reports. You will know what to expect in terms of market cycles, volatility and receive our market trend forecast.

FREE MEMBERSHIP FOR LIFE – LIMITED OFFER

Name:

Email:

Submit

Visit: www.AlgoTrades.net/monthly-investor-report/